Jesus Speaks Today

JESUS SPEAKS TODAY

John E. Hunter

BROADMAN PRESS
Nashville, Tennessee

© Copyright 1982 • Broadman Press.
All rights reserved.
4251-84
ISBN: 0-8054-5184-6

Unless otherwise marked, quotations are from the King James Version of the Bible.

Scriptures marked TEV are from the *Good News Bible*, the Bible in Today's English Version. Old Testament: Copyright © American Bible Society 1976; New Testament: Copyright © American Bible Society 1966, 1971, 1976. Used by permission.

Scriptures marked Phillips are reprinted with permission of Macmillan Publishing Co., Inc. from J. B. Phillips: *The New Testament in Modern English*, Revised Edition. © J. B. Phillips 1958, 1960, 1972.

Scriptures marked NIV are from the HOLY BIBLE *New International Version*, copyright © 1978, New York Bible Society. Used by permission.

Scriptures marked AT are the author's translations.

Dewey Decimal Classification: 232.954
Subject heading: JESUS CHRIST—TEACHINGS
Library of Congress Catalog Card Number: 81-68042
Printed in the United States of America

Contents

PART I WHAT HE SAYS 7
1. The Background 9
2. For the Bankrupt Sinner 15
3. For the Bankrupt Saint........................... 19
4. For the Brokenhearted—Healing by Sharing 24
5. For the Brokenhearted—Healing by Involvement 30
6. For the Bound 35
7. For the Blind 44
8. For the Bruised 50

PART II WHAT HE ASKS 57
9. "What Seek Ye?" 59
10. "Wilt Thou Be Made Whole?" 70
11. "Where Are the Nine?" 79
12. "Believest Thou This?" 87
13. "Why Do You Worry About the Rest?"................. 94
14. "Will You Also Go Away?" 103
15. "Why Weepest Thou?" 111

PART I
WHAT HE SAYS

1.
The Background

Some years ago I was speaking at a conference in Hamburg, Germany. I was staying in the home of German friends. As I walked in the streets near my place of residence, I came across a magnificent example of modern architecture. It looked incongruous in its setting, but the whole effect was majestic.

As I approached the building and examined it more closely, I found it was a place of Jewish worship. Later on I inquired of my hosts concerning this outstanding edifice. I was told it was erected by the German government as a mark of respect for the many Jews of Hamburg who perished in the Nazi regime.

A day or two later when I was passing the temple, I saw the janitor working on the entrance. I asked him whether I, as a Gentile, would be allowed in to witness and share the sabbath service. He told me I would be very welcome at any time. He also reminded me that all men wore a head covering in the service. I had no hat with me, but my host offered to lend me one of his. Unfortunately, his head was smaller than mine, so that wearing his hat required a delicate balancing act.

I went to the service alone, and what I witnessed was both impressive and illuminating. I saw, first of all, that the women, girls, and children were seated in an upper gallery. As far as I could tell, they took no part in the service. At times their conversations became very noisy, but no one seemed to notice or care.

The men on the lower floor were a motley and mixed group. I learned that most of them were survivors of concentration camps. They certainly appeared emaciated and obviously looked older than their years. The place of worship was very large and impressive, but the worshipers were small in number and did not look affluent.

Several boys and younger men were among the number. Each was wearing a small circular head covering, and had a shawl around his shoulders. I stood in the rear along with several other visitors. The language was unknown to me, but I listened and followed most attentively. To begin with the service dragged a little, and there was a constant stream of latecomers. As each of the late arrivals reached his place he stood, and with bowed head and hands folded in prayer, rocked to and fro on his feet. All the time he murmured words that could be heard even above the rest of the service which was then in progress.

As each latecomer was finally seated, he began rapidly reading the service from the beginning until he caught up with the tempo of worship. He then lapsed into the quiet speed of those around him. The whole service lasted over three hours, but I did not stay to the end.

The most important event of the worship service was the part that really came alive to me. After many minutes of quiet, subdued reading and repetition, the whole congregation suddenly took on a new and vibrant involvement. The leader in charge on the platform walked slowly, and with measured dignity, to two doors set at shoulder level at the back of the stage. As he began to open the doors, the men in the congregation became extremely enthusiastic. Cries of "Hallelujah" and "Shalom" were heard all around me—plus other expressions of joy and adoration.

The leader then took out of the cupboard behind the doors a very ornate object. I learned later that this was the Torah—the Word of God—written on a large roll which was encased in a beautifully embroidered container. As he stepped forward with the Torah over his shoulder, the temple was filled with increasing shouts of adoration. A mounting sense of excitement filled the place.

The leader came down from the platform and began a slow, dignified walk up and down all the walkways in the hall. As he did so, men of all ages left their seats and moved towards him. With tears streaming down their faces, these men would kiss the shawl over their shoulders and then press the kiss against the beautiful container. This was a very moving spectacle.

As the Torah passed each row, the men, having demonstrated their love for God's Word, then sat quietly on their seats with heads bowed and bodies swaying to and fro.

THE BACKGROUND

When the procession finally ended, the leader returned to the platform. In the center of the stage was a large reading desk—similar to the pulpit or podium in a Christian church. I soon realized why this desk was much larger than a normal pulpit.

With great reverence, the leader removed the covering from the roll, revealing the Torah itself—the written Word of God. This ritual brought further outbursts of adoration from the already excited men.

Suddenly the place was quiet! The contrast to the previous joyous involvement was uncanny. The moment had come for the great event—the reading of the Word of God!

At this point I, too, became most interested, because I was seeing history take place before my very eyes. Placing the large roll on the larger desk, the leader slowly and reverently unwound it until he found the place with the marker indicating where the reading had ended during the previous service.

Having found the place, he then went on to choose the person to do the reading. At this point every man was looking up at him in hopeful expectation. One man was to be chosen—what an honor this would be! His privilege would be to read God's Word and to make a few comments on it. The men waited as the eyes of the leader traveled around the congregation. Eventually he saw someone who satisfied his standards, and he called out the man's name. A sigh moved across the whole audience as man after man registered disappointment or envy of the one chosen.

The one called stood with bursting delight and moved with great solemnity to the platform. The leader showed him where to begin the reading; then the reader raised his voice, and a holy hush filled the place as the sacred words were spoken once again. Suddenly he stopped, replaced the marker, and having rerolled the Torah, he handed it back to the leader. It was now his privilege and opportunity to speak a few words of comment, after which he returned to his seat—the envy of every man in the building.

The service continued, and soon afterward I made a quick exit, leaving this moment of sacred history to enter once more the busy world—a world too busy for God.

Later on, as I meditated on what I had seen and shared, I realized in a new and wonderful way what had actually happened on the day recorded for us in Luke 4:16-22. "And he came to Nazareth, where he had been brought up: and, as his custom was, he went into the synagogue on the sabbath day, and stood up for the read" (v. 16). The events recorded here follow the temptation of our Lord in the wilderness, which itself followed his baptism as set forth in Luke 3:21-22.

Luke 4 begins, "And Jesus being full of the Holy Ghost returned from Jordan, and was led by the Spirit into the wilderness, Being forty days tempted of the devil" (vv. 1-2a). The beginning of the Lord's ministry is seen in verse 14, "And Jesus returned in the power of the Spirit into Galilee: and there went out a fame of him through all the region round about."

Notice that it is no sin to be tempted. The Lord was tempted forty days, yet without sin. Temptation when resisted in the fullness of the Spirit can, of itself, produce a new power of the Spirit.

Our Lord went on in the power of the Spirit, and his journey took him to Nazareth, his hometown.

It comes as a surprise to many people to find out where our Lord sat when he went to "church." He was the carpenter of Nazareth, a skilled craftsman, but not a member of the priestly families. As a result, his place was in the congregation, certainly not at the pulpit.

The service in the Nazareth synagogue that special sabbath morning would be very similar to the one I attended in Hamburg, especially the part about the reading of the Word of God. As at Hamburg, the leader would look around his congregation to see whom he would choose to read the Scriptures. His eyes would light on Jesus, the carpenter, whose fame as a teacher and a prophet was beginning to spread through all the region round about.

Thus it was that he would invite Jesus to come to the reading desk, giving our Lord the honor of reading the portion of Scripture set for that day. Verse 17 says, "And there was delivered unto him the book of the prophet Esaias [Isaiah]. And when he had opened the book, he found the place where it is written."

Remembering the incident at Hamburg, it is important to realize that Jesus did not select those particular verses from which he read. Whoever had been chosen that morning would have read those same words. "He found the place" tells us that the previous reading stopped just before this passage.

This whole incident was one of those minor miracles in the Word

THE BACKGROUND

of God. Notice what Jesus read: "The Spirit of the Lord is upon me, because he hath anointed me to preach the gospel to the poor; he hath sent me to heal the brokenhearted, to preach deliverance to the captives, and recovering of sight to the blind, to set at liberty them that are bruised, To preach the acceptable year of the Lord" (vv. 18-19).

After this reading he closed the book; that is, he rolled up the Torah and gave it again to the minister.

There are some remarkable features about this special reading. Notice first how short it was. In our translation, there is just one sentence. This is surely far too short for a Bible reading.

But then compare the passage read by our Lord and the original as set forth in Isaiah 61:1-2. We will find that he stopped in the middle of a sentence and ended his reading at a comma.

Looking at the original, we find that the next words to be read were "and the day of vengeance of our God" (Isa. 61:2).

That "day of vengeance" will surely come, and the One in control will be our Lord himself, but that day has not yet arrived. It is still the day of grace for 'whosoever will.'

Had our Lord continued his reading, even to the completing of verse 2, there would be no hope for any of us. As it was, he stopped halfway. Thank God, Jesus never finished his sentence. "The unfinished sentence" is the only hope for this poor, torn world.

The man in Hamburg was allowed to make a few comments on his reading. It was even so with Jesus. After he had returned the roll to the minister we read, "And the eyes of all them that were in the synagogue were fastened on him" (v. 20). The word translated "fastened" is a powerful word. *Vine's Expository Dictionary* says, "It always has a strongly intensive meaning." The power of the Spirit was very evident that sabbath morning as our Lord finished reading his one sentence. His comment was one of the greatest things he ever said: "This day is this scripture fulfilled in your ears" (v. 21).

Those precious words had stood for hundreds of years, in Isaiah, a promise to the many in need and now, on that special day, they were fulfilled.

This is really the reason for this book, *Jesus Speaks Today*. I have come to realize, as never before, the urgency of the need of a Savior who is available day by day. It is indeed tremendous to know my sins

are forgiven and to be quietly confident of a home in heaven, but I have met so many believers who, knowing all this, are beset with problems and fears completely beyond their capacity vto handle.
What we are seeking in this volume is the reality of a Savior who is "still in business."
During that same visit to Hamburg, I spoke to a college group of believers. All of them were saved, but that was not enough. In a question and answer session the leader suddenly cried out in a voice full of despair: "I know my sins are forgiven. I know I have a home in heaven, but can Jesus do anything for me today?" The whole group voiced a total agreement with that question.
This is the cry, often the silent one, of many all over the world. "Can Jesus do anything for me today?" This may be your own specific need. If this is so, I have good news for you. I want to tell you more about these five special areas of weakness and need of which our Lord spoke. Remember, he said: "This day is this scripture fulfilled in your ears." Ever since that blessed sabbath day in the synagogue at Nazareth, the Lord has been doing exactly what he said he would.
I have seen him do it. I have experienced his mighty power. I know he can do much for you whoever you are, whatever your need may be.
So come with me and let me introduce you to my Lord. Let us examine each of these five special groups of people, and you will find your place as you wait on him, and for him.

2.
For the Bankrupt Sinner

The first words read by Jesus in the synagogue that day were: "The Spirit of the Lord is upon me, because he hath anointed me to preach the gospel to the poor" (Luke 4:18). The word *gospel* actually means "good news." So the first group to be blessed are the poor, and for them there is good news.

There are a lot of poor people in the world today. I meet them wherever I go—in Africa, South America, India, The Philippines, and also in the Far East. We talk about the poor in the United States, but many of those are rich compared to the hopelessly poor of other nations.

But there is one thing worse than being poor—that is to be bankrupt! It is possible to be poor and yet make ends meet. There are many people alive today who went through the Great Depression of the late 1920's and early 1930's. They were poor and yet held their heads high and eventually made a financial success in life.

But bankruptcy is something far worse than poverty. Bankruptcy means having debts to pay, but possessing no means of meeting those debts. It means being below the poverty level, losing self-respect, being an acknowledged failure, with no possible way out. You are just bankrupt.

This is how we all are in the sight of the Holy God—totally bankrupt. We have debts to pay, sins for which to atone, guilt to be dealt with—but none of us has the slightest shred of anything to offer.

In this chapter, I want to consider the bankrupt sinner and how he or she stands in the sight of a holy God.

I never heard the gospel, to be affected by it, until I was in my early twenties. I lived in England at that time. I was white, had finished college, was in my first teaching position, and I would have called myself a Christian—because of the facts stated above.

Then I heard the message of the gospel. The preacher was talking about sinners, and I believed in sinners. They were people who robbed, killed, and broke the law—but I was not that kind of a person. I thought I was good and always on the side of the law.

I remember looking around the congregation that first time and wondering who the sinners were to whom the preacher was addressing his remarks. I noticed one or two doubtful-looking characters in the congregation, and asked my friend if they were the sinners. To my surprise, I was told they were deacons!

Fortunately, I continued to attend the church, and so continued to hear the gospel. Very soon the Holy Spirit began to convict me, and in my own heart I knew something was wrong. At first I was put off by the words in Romans 3:23: "For all have sinned, and come short of the glory of God"—especially the "all have sinned" part. Because I had not broken the law openly, I counted myself out of that classification. Then I began to realize I was a sinner not because of what I had done, but because of what I had not done. I had not reached God's standard.

There may be someone reading these words who also rebels against the idea that "all have sinned." Let me show you how it came clear to me. Little by little I began to see that God had a standard. In one sense, that standard was the perfect life of Christ. When I measured my life against his holy, sinless life, I could see immediately that I came short. The evil, wicked people came short, too. They came a long way short. Now I wasn't evil or wicked, but I also came short—not as short as the bad people but I came short, and that made me a sinner. In this way I could understand and agree that "all have sinned, and come short of the glory of God."

The most beautiful, sacrificial life ever lived somehow, somewhere, someway, comes short of the glory of God—and, so, "all have sinned." This is what makes one a sinner in the sight of God, although in the eyes of the world one may be a splendid person, a fine citizen, or a successful business person.

As soon as I realized I was a sinner, I knew I was in trouble, because I had no means of paying for my sin. Previously in my thinking I had assumed that if I did my best and lived a "good" life I would, somehow, be all right in the end. This vague philosophy was shared by others whom I knew.

But having accepted the fact that I was a sinner, I now had no "good" life with which to pay for my sins. Just as a criminal in the courts cannot forgive his own crimes, I could not forgive my own sins, or work out my own forgiveness. Because of this I was bankrupt. I had debts to pay but no means to meet those payments. And so it is with you, my friend, if you have not found God's answer to your sin and guilt.

This is where those first words of Jesus come as a gleam of hope in the silence of sin. Our Lord read and said, "He hath anointed me to preach the gospel to the poor"—good news to the poor, better news for the bankrupt. There is a way of meeting all our debts and dealing with the hideous question of guilt. This is made so wonderfully clear when we read in 1 Peter 2:24, "Who his own self bare our sins in his own body on the tree, that we, being dead to sins, should live unto righteousness; by whose stripes ye were healed." Notice those two parallel phrases—"his own self . . . his own body." Because of his own personal involvement, all our sins have been dealt with. That which we could not meet because of our bankruptcy has been fully paid for by the blood shed at Calvary: "Forasmuch as ye know that ye were not redeemed with corruptible things . . . but with the precious blood of Christ, as of a lamb without blemish and without spot" (1 Pet. 1:18-19).

All that God requires from me is an open admission of my bankruptcy and an open confession to him of my sin. "If we confess our sins, he is faithful and just to forgive us our sins, and to cleanse us from all unrighteousness" (1 John 1:9).

This is surely good news for the bankrupt sinner. I know it was for me when I accepted Christ as my own personal Savior. Not only were my sins forgiven, but I was cleansed from all guilt. Such a situation is almost too marvelous even to begin to consider, and yet it is all true.

Some people, of course, refuse to recognize this bankruptcy. They rationalize their acts to do away with sin and guilt. They seek to pretend that they can "pay their own way." The only trouble is their currency is not acceptable in heaven. What they consider good works on earth are looked on as "filthy rags" (Isa. 64:6) in heaven. Only one currency is acceptable to meet the bankruptcy of sin: "By the which will we are sanctified through the offering of the body of Jesus Christ once for all" (Heb. 10:10).

Jesus said: "I am the way, the truth, and the life: no man cometh unto the Father but by me" (John 14:6).

May I counsel you, if you are still in a state of spiritual bankruptcy, to turn to the Lord now. Acknowledge your hopeless situation and seek to use all that the Lord has provided so that you can move from a state of bankruptcy to a state of blessedness.

A Prayer for a Bankrupt Sinner

Heavenly Father, I have heard your word, I believe your word, and I acknowledge my utter bankruptcy. I am a sinner with no means of my own to meet the claims you have against me as the Holy God.

But, Heavenly Father, I believe Jesus died for sinners. Therefore he died for me. I believe he bore my sins in his own body to the cross. I believe Jesus paid it all. I believe you will not demand a further payment from me.

Therefore I thank you for this good news for the bankrupt sinner. Thank you, Lord Jesus, for forgiveness; thank you for cleansing.

Thank you my bankruptcy is ended, and I am accepted in the Beloved One.

3.
For the Bankrupt Saint

The words "The Bankrupt Saint" seem contradictory. How can a saint be bankrupt?

Let me say right away that the word *saint* as used here does not in any way refer to especially selected beings to whom special prayer is made. In the Bible, the word *saint* indicates the ordinary believer, one who is "separate, set apart for God." "To all that be in Rome, beloved of God, called to be saints" (Rom. 1:7). "Unto the church of God which is at Corinth, to them that are sanctified [set apart] in Christ Jesus, called to be saints" (1 Cor. 1:2). "Paul, an apostle of Jesus Christ by the will of God, to the saints which are at Ephesus" (Eph. 1:1).

Talking about a bankrupt saint is almost the same as talking about a bankrupt millionaire. How can a man possessing great financial wealth be bankrupt? It sounds impossible, but it can be tragically true. Just last week I saw in a newspaper the strange story of an elderly woman who had starved to death, and all the time she possessed great wealth. We call such people eccentrics. They choose to live miserable, pitiful lives when they have sufficient resources to enjoy comfort and pleasure.

Strange as it may seem, there are many "spiritual eccentrics," people who choose to live miserable, pitiful lives when they possess sufficient resources to enjoy a good life, full of joy and quiet satisfaction.

Recently in my devotions I was reading these words from 2 Corinthians 9:8, "And God is able to make all grace abound toward you; that ye, always having all sufficiency in all things, may abound to every good work." What an amazing verse this is—always having all grace that gives "all sufficiency in all things." Do you believe it? Did God *really* mean it—or was he just exaggerating a little?

I am confident it means what it says. I have proved it to mean what it says. The Word of God backs up every word in that promise. Every true believer always has resources available to meet any and every need—whatever that need may be!

The trouble with many people is that they believe and accept such verses, but they limit them only to special areas of need. If it can be classified as a "religious" situation, then we look to the Lord to deal with it. But if it concerns our ordinary everyday lives—domestic life, financial need, health, business, children, and so on—we choose to assume responsibility for that area. With all the miserable poverty of our fallen human natures, we move in to handle the situation. We are bankrupt before we begin; no wonder we are broken as we continue!

In many cases, the spiritual bankruptcy is the result of "backsliding"—the term we apply to getting away from God in thought, word, and deed. In other cases it is due to what I call "honest ignorance." It was so in my own personal life. I knew enough of the teaching of the Word of God to bring me forgiveness of my sins and to guarantee a home in heaven, but I never knew the teaching regarding coping with life day by day. I was fit to die and go to heaven as a forgiven sinner, but I was not fit to live as a forgiven saint!

Sometimes it seems to me that the devil deliberately seeks to limit the believer's knowledge of the truth of God's Word, as if he cannot keep us from being saved, but he can and does stop us from going on to know the fullness of our salvation.

Every believer knows the truth of the death of Christ, of how he bore our sins in his own body on the cross, as we studied in chapter 1. But I am discovering that there are thousands who do not know the truth of the life of Christ.

God's salvation is like a precious coin from heaven, minted by mercy on the throne of grace. Every earthly coin has two sides. If a side is missing, or is defaced, then it is not legal tender.

It is so with the coin of our salvation. The Lord Jesus once asked concerning a human coin, "Whose image and superscription hath it?" (Luke 20:24). To continue our imagery of the coin of salvation, we could likewise ask whose image it bears. We would discover that just as a coin has two sides, so our coin of salvation presents two aspects of our Lord in his great work of redemption.

One side depicts the death of Christ, revealing how our sins are forgiven through his precious shed blood. The other side depicts the saving life of Christ which tells of his present work for the believer. His death is the finished work of Christ. His life tells of his indwelling Holy Spirit—indwelling each believer and making us the recipients of his risen life and power, a moment by moment experience.

Acts 13:14 begins the story of the time Paul preached in Antioch in Pisidia. In verse 16 we read, "Then Paul stood up, and beckoning with his hand said, Men of Israel, and ye that fear God, give audience." Notice he was addressing himself to both the Jews and the Gentiles. He went on to tell how our Lord was crucified: "But God raised him from the dead. . . . And we declare unto you glad tidings, how that the promise which was made unto the fathers, God hath fulfilled the same unto us their children, in that he hath raised up Jesus again; as it is also written in the second psalm, Thou art my Son, this day have I begotten thee" (vv. 30,32-33).

Notice the vital importance of these words, as directed by the Holy Spirit: The promise of salvation was fulfilled in the risen Christ. The promise was not fulfilled at the cross. It was fulfilled in the risen, victorious Christ.

If we examine the preaching of the gospel as recorded in the days of the early church, we will find the final emphasis always to be on the risen Christ. They offered to men and women a relationship with a living person who would come and indwell them by his Holy Spirit.

By contrast, much of our evangelism today centers on the cross—thank God a million times that the cross is so uplifted—but the pity is that this is where it centers and ceases. We offer to men and women a Savior who died for them. By his shed blood they have forgiveness of sins and a home in heaven. All this is wonderfully true, but it is only one side of the coin of salvation.

Paul offered a risen Christ indwelling each saint by his Holy Spirit as the other side of the coin. It is possible to preach the cross without emphasizing the purpose and power of the resurrection, but when the final emphasis is on the resurrection the cross is fully dealt with.

This brings me back to a statement I made previously. Spiritual bankruptcy is due in many cases to honest ignorance. This honest ignorance concerns the other side of the coin. We know the teaching concerning the death of Christ, but we are ignorant about his saving life.

Paul always spoke of himself and his faith in terms of his relationship to that risen Lord. "That I may know him, and the power of his resurrection" (Phil. 3:10). "For to me to live is Christ, and to die is gain" (Phil. 1:21). "I can do all things through Christ which strengtheneth me" (Phil. 4:13). "The mystery which hath been hid from ages and from generations, . . . the riches of the glory of this mystery . . . which is Christ in you, the hope of glory" (Col. 1:26-27).

If you are a believer then you are already indwelt by Christ, through his Holy Spirit. You do not have to ask for the Holy Spirit. He is already there, within you.

The verse that made saving sense to me when I was converted was Revelation 3:20, "Behold, I stand at the door, and knock: if any man hear my voice, and open the door, I will come in to him, and will sup with him, and he with me." I heard him knocking on the door of my life. I opened that door, and he came in, in the person and power of his Holy Spirit.

If you have not opened your heart's door to him, the following verse applies to you: "Now if any man have not the Spirit of Christ, he is none of his" (Rom. 8:9). Conversely, if at any time you open your life to Christ, you can realize that he will never leave you nor forsake you. Always remember that the moment you were saved you received the Holy Spirit. Otherwise you would be "none of his."

But knowing the *fact* of the indwelling Christ does not bring vitality to my vision. I can believe that Christ indwells me. I can recite all the Scriptures to verify my belief. But unless I can turn belief into behavior, my daily experience will be one of spiritual bankruptcy. I will be like the millionaire who possessed great riches, yet lived in self-imposed poverty.

It was a great day for me when I realized my total bankruptcy, when I understood that because of my fallen human nature God expected nothing of me but failure. It was then that I began to see for the first time the full significance of the presence of the risen, victorious Christ in my life. I, too, can do all things through Christ. God has no favorites; he never gave to Paul more than he gave to me.

Paul could say: "I know whom I have believed" (2 Tim. 1:12). I also know whom I have believed. If you are a true believer you also know whom you have believed. But I am learning more than ever that it is not what you know that really counts, but what you do with what you know.

Knowing Christ as your own personal Savior makes you a spiritual millionaire, full of the riches of his grace. But living only in the good of his death leaves me a spiritual bankrupt, using only one side of the coin of salvation.

The Bible is full of exhortations to go on with Christ. "As ye have therefore received Christ Jesus the Lord, so walk ye in him" (Col. 2:6). I begin with his saving death; I go on with his saving life. "As you have received . . . so walk." I walk, receiving all that he is for all that I need, and I walk by faith.

At the cross I committed to him the whole question of my sin. In the crisis, I commit to him the whole question of my self, my total inability to cope with life, my fears, frustrations, the bitter bankruptcy of my fallen human nature.

I learned to say, by faith, "Lord Jesus, I cannot handle this situation, face this fear, meet this crisis. I cannot, but you can. That is why you came to indwell me. Your total sufficiency is the continual answer to my failure."

See yourself in relation to Luke 4:18: "He hath anointed me to preach the gospel to the poor"—good news for the poor, better news for the bankrupt. Step, by faith, into all the riches of his grace and learn to live like a child of the King.

Prayer for a Bankrupt Saint

Heavenly Father, I have already thanked you for the wonder of my salvation, for the sure knowledge that Jesus died for me on the cross.

Now, dear Lord, I want to thank you that he did not only die for me on the cross, but now he lives in me and for me in the crises of life.

I thank you that Jesus indwells me by his Holy Spirit. He who possesses all power in heaven and on earth will never leave nor forsake me.

How rich I am! All grace is mine. I always have all sufficiency in all things. This is the answer to my failure and my bankruptcy. Help me now to live in the good of that glorious sufficiency. As I have received, so may I walk: in his power, for his sake.

4.
For the Brokenhearted — Healing by Sharing

I am writing this chapter in my home in England. I have just returned from a visit to the United States. Last week I was in Florida. It was March, and the temperature was in the low eighties. They warned us of a coming "low" of fifty-seven! Here in England it is bitterly cold. There is a rainstorm beating on my window, and hail is rattling like machine-gun fire on every exposed place.

In a short while we will be leaving to attend a funeral. What a day for a funeral! A good friend of ours is mourning the death of his wife. She had a long, drawn-out, painful death, and he is such a quiet, gentle soul. I know he is brokenhearted. When I see him, I will try to say some kind words to him, but nothing that I can say will heal his broken heart.

Fortunately, he knows and loves the Lord Jesus. His whole family are sincere believers. So the best I can do is to commit and commend him to the one who said, "He hath sent me to heal the brokenhearted" (Luke 4:18).

Thank God there is someone who can heal broken hearts, because there are many today. Wherever I go I meet them. They are all races, all ages, and they suffer for many different reasons. But they all feel that dull, inward pain of inexpressible bewilderment that comes from a broken heart.

When one has a broken limb, everyone around can tell by the cast or bandage, and sympathy and consideration are shown in the appropriate way. But, often there is no obvious evidence of a broken heart — no cast, crutch, bandage, or sling — just the numbness of bitterness, the emptiness of loneliness. Even when we know of another's suffering, the best we can offer is a kindly phrase, a sympathetic look, or the gentle touch of a hand — so inadequate.

How satisfying it is to read those words again in Luke 4:18: "He

FOR THE BROKENHEARTED—HEALING BY SHARING

hath sent me to heal the brokenhearted"—with the blessed assurance that "This day is this scripture fulfilled in your ears" (v. 21).

I am praying that this chapter will come to someone in need as from the Lord himself. I would love to speak these words to you in person, with an earnestness that would reach you in your hurt condition.

Please realize that our Lord said he was sent to heal the brokenhearted. The emphasis is on the word "heal." He did not promise to "cheer up," or "patch up," or "take your mind off it," but to bring a definite healing so that the hurt is gone and the wound is closed forever! Only Jesus can do this. This is one of the precious ministries of the risen victorious Christ as he indwells you by his Holy Spirit.

When he was here on earth, his whole ministry was geared to such a precious purpose. Recall how his heart went out, especially to women in utter distress. The woman with the issue of blood for twelve years heard him say: "Daughter, be of good comfort: thy faith hath made thee whole; go in peace" (Luke 8:48). The widow of Nain who had just lost her only son experienced this: "And when the Lord saw her, he had compassion on her, and said unto her, Weep not. . . . And he delivered him to his mother" (Luke 7:13,15). Consider the utter shame of the woman taken in adultery, exposed to the leers of the "holy" men. Think how they all "went out one by one," until only Jesus was left to say, "Neither do I condemn thee: go, and sin no more" (John 8:11). Even as he hung dying on the cross, his eyes took in the bitter, hopeless loneliness of his own mother, and his thoughts were for her protection: "Woman, behold thy son" (John 19:26).

He is "Jesus Christ [he himself] the same yesterday, and to-day, and for ever" (Heb. 13:8). What he ever was, he ever is. What he ever did, he ever does—even today in the midst of your hurt and brokenness.

I want to tell you of two ways in which our Lord can heal the brokenhearted. First let me share with you the wonderful words of 2 Corinthians 1:3-4: "Blessed be God, even the Father of our Lord Jesus Christ, the Father of mercies, and the God of all comfort: Who comforteth us in all our tribulation, that we may be able to comfort them which are in any trouble, by the comfort wherewith we ourselves are comforted of God." This is surely one of the most comforting verses in the whole Bible—five times the emphasis is placed on this blessed ministry of our loving God.

We talk about comforting people, by which we mean saying kind words to help them in their distress. This is usually the most we can do.

But the word *comfort* used in these verses has a positive, powerful meaning. There is nothing insipid or weak about it. The basic word is *fort*, which means strength. Many towns in the United States have the word *Fort* in their names—Fort Worth, Fort Collins. They were originally the strong places in the midst of hostile, dangerous territory. In them the United States Cavalry was based. To them the early settlers would go for shelter. From them the same cavalry would go out to subdue the enemy.

"Comfort" means to pour in strength, to come with added support, to bring new resources to areas of weakness. In John 14, 15, and 16 our Lord himself spoke four times of the Holy Spirit as the Comforter—the One who comes alongside to be our strength.

Realizing this positive meaning, see now how he is the God of all comfort. No one else can comfort like he can, because no one else has the capacity to comfort. Then notice that he comforts us in all our tribulations. This word *tribulation* is another good word to study. The basic word here is *tribulum*. A *tribulum* was a Roman agricultural implement used in the threshing of wheat. It consisted of two wooden poles, one about five feet tall, the other about four feet tall. The poles were joined together with a leather hinge at one end. I was in Racine, Wisconsin, some time ago and visited the folk museum there. I was surprised to see a tribulum among the tools used by the early settlers.

The wheat was gathered in a heap on the barn, or garner, floor, and around it stood a group of muscular men each armed with a tribulum. When threshing began, the workmen in turn held the long pole over the shoulder, then swung up the shorter pole to bring it down with a steady blow on the wheat. This became a continuous series of blows aimed at one place, for the purpose of releasing the grains of wheat.

It is from this continual series of blows falling on the one place that we get the present word *tribulation*. Tribulation in human experience may draw no blood, nor break any bones. It can be just one event after another beating on the heart and life of a person, crushing one to the ground with the intensity of tragedy.

FOR THE BROKENHEARTED—HEALING BY SHARING

This is where the God of all comfort comes with his mighty power. The believer, as we saw in chapter 3, possesses the wondrous presence of the risen Lord Jesus, who, in turn, possesses all power in heaven and on earth. As we come with our tribulation, helpless and brokenhearted, and open up the whole situation to him, he will then pour in unlimited strength.

The whole secret is opening up the whole situation to him. Often we try to be brave and carry the load ourselves. We feel we would be letting the Lord down if we did not suffer for his sake. But that is just what Satan would have us do, to stand in our own strength in the face of such tragedy.

The more we try to bear our burdens by ourselves, the more we cut ourselves off from the comfort of God. Think back over the many stories of blessing in the Gospel narratives. In each case the sufferer came to our Lord. We mentioned earlier the woman who touched the hem of his garment. She did so in faith and was healed. In fact, our Lord said, "Thy faith hath made thee whole." There were many more lame people who were never healed, many more blind who never saw, many lepers who remained in their destitution, simply because when Jesus was available they never opened up their situations to him.

In like manner, there are many believers today who bear the burden of a broken heart because they either do not know of his comfort, or they will not keep on opening up the whole situation to him by faith.

Thus the first blessing in these verses is to experience the comfort of God. But it does not stop there: "That we may be able to comfort them which are in any trouble, by the comfort wherewith we ourselves are comforted of God." The real healing begins when we go on to share that comfort with others.

It is not enough just to receive the blessing. The true work of healing proceeds when we share with others in their sorrows the peace which has filled our own hearts.

This is pictured for us in the comparison of the two seas—the Sea of Galilee and the Dead Sea. The Jordan River flows into the Sea of Galilee, bringing the fresh, sparkling water which produces an abundance of life—fish in the sea and vegetation around. But the water does not stay there. It flows in and continues out, speeding on its way to the Dead Sea. The same water that brings life to Galilee enters the Dead Sea, and there it stops. There is no way out. Because there is no sharing of the living water, there is no life either in or around the Dead Sea, hence its name. There is no healing as in Galilee, because there is no sharing as in Galilee.

This could be the reason why some believers never experience the full healing of a broken heart. They have been eager to experience the comfort of God, but slow to share that blessing with others in their particular needs.

In recent years, my wife and I have learned the truth of this message concerning the comfort of God, experienced and shared, through the bitter tragedy of one who is dear to us. She is a Christian who was married for nearly fifteen years before the repeated blows of tribulation brought her to brokenness. Her husband, a Christian who was never a strong character, developed a craving for drugs—tranquilizers and "pep" pills. His addiction was such that his personality began to deteriorate rapidly. To make matters worse, he began to be dependent on a psychiatrist who encouraged him in un-Christlike behavior. He also had several electric shock treatments, which seemed to make him more unbalanced than ever.

He was encouraged to persecute his wife in order to relieve his own tensions. This he did by spreading malicious and horrible stories, all designed to ruin her character and reveal him as the injured party. He had great success in this area, visiting his many Christian friends and feeding into their minds the filth of his sick mind. It was sad to see how so many people believed all he said without ever testing what was told or hearing the other side of the story.

Eventually, he found another woman who promised to marry him if he would divorce his wife. All his efforts were then directed to getting a divorce.

At first, his wife was ignorant of his talebearing. Then she refused to descend to his level—believing the Lord would vindicate her. In the end, she agreed not to contest the divorce—refusing to go to law before the unbelievers (1 Cor. 6:1). As soon as possible, the husband married the other woman. Nineteen days later he took his own life!

Before he remarried, he made a will leaving all his possessions to his two sons, but he did not know that the law of England states that when a man remarries all his previous wills become invalid. The first wife was left with nothing, and the other woman came into his fortune.

One of the sons was an acute diabetic, thirteen years old. The other was a nervous boy of eleven. All these events happened over a period of three years and were worsened by her utter poverty—a vivid example of tribulation. The poor wife was left crushed, brokenhearted, and numb with shock. Added to all this was the stigma of divorce, the suffering of rejection, plus the fact that his foul stories were accepted as truth.

The one bright part in this miserable epic is the way the forsaken wife turned to the Lord. She learned little by little, and often through great heartache, that the Lord Jesus was the only one who could pour in strength. As she opened up the whole vast area of need and suffering to him, he, in turn, became increasingly real to her.

She was soon to find that she was only one of many in our small town of twenty thousand whose hearts were broken with sorrow and tragedy. The Lord led her on to share with others the comfort wherewith she had been comforted by him. In this way, she became a channel of blessing to others. But the glorious fact is that she has experienced healing in depth. He who said he came to heal the brokenhearted has done just what he said he would, because first she experienced the comfort of God and then she shared with others the blessed peace of his presence.

Always remember that God has no favorites. What he does for one of his children he will do for others, if they do what his word instructs.

You may be one of those brokenhearted people, bewildered, rejected, and with that dull, inner pain of hopelessness. Why don't you open up the whole situation to the one who said he was sent to heal the brokenhearted?

A Prayer for the Brokenhearted

Dear God, is this really true? Can you heal a broken heart?

Dare I come to you with my hopeless need? I want to spread the whole wretched situation before you.

If you were sent to heal the brokenhearted, please come and make yourself real to me. Show me how to open up the whole situation. Pour in your strength.

Then, Lord, lead me to others who need to know you, and whose hearts are hurting, and let me share your comfort.

Thank you. You are "Jesus Christ the same [he himself] yesterday, and today, and for ever."

5.
For the Brokenhearted — Healing by Involvement

In this chapter I want us to see another way in which the Lord Jesus fulfills his promise to heal the brokenhearted.

On the 19th of July in AD 64, there was a great fire in the city of Rome. The emperor at that time was Nero, who showed signs of being mentally deranged. This is the incident which is associated with the story of "Nero fiddling while Rome was burning."

The area destroyed by fire was the ghetto where many poor people lived. This area was adjoining Nero's great palace, and the verdict of history is that Nero instigated the fire so that he could extend his palace grounds. As the fire raged, the people fled from their homes. When they returned to the ghetto, they found the whole area was closed off, to be included in the palace property.

Not only did the people lose their possessions, they also lost their property. Naturally, someone had to be blamed for the fire — but whom? It would be suicide to blame Nero — then whom?

It so happened that rumors began to spread concerning a new secret society in Rome — people who were called Christians. No one knew much about them. Their God was never seen, as were the other gods of Rome. Then, too, it was mostly the poor and slaves who belonged to the group. This was not an impressive way to begin a new society. In any case, secret societies are always suspect in a totalitarian state, and Rome was the perfect example of such an organization, complete with secret police and a mad dictator.

Thus it was that eventually the Christians were blamed for the destruction. A people who were reported to eat human flesh and drink human blood at their secret meetings could be capable of any other antisocial activity. The story of the flesh and blood came from a distortion of the communion service. Our Lord said, "Take, eat; this is my body. . . . Drink ye all of it; For this is my blood of the new testament" (Matt. 26:26-28).

Pinning the blame on the Christians was a double blessing to Nero. First, it absolved him from the crime. Also, punishing the "criminals" gave him an excellent opportunity to divert the growing public antagonism to his regime. Using the execution of Christians as a public means of entertainment satisfied everyone, except the believers.

One can go today to the Coliseum in Rome and sit in the actual seats where the spectators witnessed the suffering and tragedy of God's people. They were torn by wild animals, burned alive, and subjected to evil and filthy indignities—all to provide entertainment for the degenerate Roman society.

This policy involved the persecution and destruction of the Christians in Rome. During this period Peter himself was put to death. As time went on, more victims were needed to play their part in this degrading spectacle. Thus it was that search parties were sent out from Rome to the smaller surrounding towns to find and capture Christians—regardless of sex and age.

It is easy to realize that such a time was one of great heartache and fear for the believers. Whole families were captured, separated, tortured, and finally put to death.

One of the reasons for the two Epistles of Peter was to prepare the hearts of God's people for such future destruction. This is why we read such passages as, "For what glory is it, if, when ye be buffeted for your faults, ye shall take it patiently? but if, when ye do well, and suffer for it, ye take it patiently, this is acceptable with God. For even hereunto were ye called: because Christ also suffered for us, leaving us an example, that ye should follow his steps" (1 Pet. 2:20-21).

"But and if ye suffer for righteousness' sake, happy are ye: and be not afraid of their terror, neither be troubled" (1 Pet. 3:14).

"For it is better, if the will of God be so, that ye suffer for well-doing, than for evil-doing. For Christ also hath once suffered for sins" (1 Pet. 3:17-18).

"Forasmuch then as Christ hath suffered for us in the flesh, arm yourselves likewise with the same mind: for he that hath suffered in the flesh hath ceased from sin" (1 Pet. 4:1).

"Beloved, think it not strange concerning the fiery trial which is to try you, as though some strange thing happened unto you: But rejoice, inasmuch as ye are partakers of Christ's sufferings" (1 Pet. 4:12-13).

"If any man suffer as a Christian, let him not be ashamed; but let him glorify God on this behalf" (1 Pet. 4:16).

"Casting all your care upon him: for he careth for you" (1 Pet. 5:7).

Notice the emphasis on the word *suffering*. There was no thought of avoiding it. The main emphasis was to find a source of strength which would undergird the believer and enable him or her to cope with any form of suffering.

Be sure you see in all this the deep concern for healing the brokenhearted. Realize that these dear people, above all others, were in dire need of a healing which would equip them to stand true and firm to the end.

I want to turn your special attention to the vital words in 1 Peter 5:10: "But the God of all grace, who hath called us unto his eternal glory by Christ Jesus, after that ye have suffered a while, make you perfect, stablish, strengthen, settle you."

In the previous chapter it was "The God of all comfort" (2 Cor. 1:3) who was going to pour in strength. We saw that healing came, first, through experiencing the comfort of God, then, through sharing the comfort of God.

In this verse we will find what special blessing comes through "the God of all grace."

Four experiences of blessing are listed: 1. "make you perfect"; 2. "stablish"; 3. "strengthen"; 4. "settle you." But notice when the actual blessing takes place, it is not promised *before* the suffering, or even *during* the suffering—it is "after that ye have suffered a while." The same promise is given in Hebrews 12:11: "Now no chastening for the present seemeth to be joyous, but grievous: nevertheless afterward it yieldeth the peaceable fruit of righteousness unto them which are exercised thereby."

There is a most encouraging thought in connection with the first blessing promised, "make you perfect." First, realize that the word *perfect* does not mean "sinlessly perfect." A better translation would be, "make you complete, or adequate." But the best interpretation comes from a comparison with Mark 1:19. This particular verse records how our Lord called his disciples. Previous to verse 19 he called Simon and Andrew. In verse 19 we read, "He saw James the son of Zebedee, and John his brother, who also were in the ship mending their nets."

The word in the original translated here as "mending their nets" is the same word used in 1 Peter for "make you perfect." This gives a totally different slant to the picture. I am not being made perfect to experience a spiritual peak, but for a purpose I undertake.

Somehow, in the economy of God, the suffering, brokenhearted believer who responds to the call of the Lord will experience the healing promised through an involvement with the risen Christ.

The God of all grace will "mend my nets," thus equipping me for future service. It is a known fact that somehow the Lord can use a brokenhearted believer who has experienced healing in a unique way. Such precious souls are outstanding first for their suffering, then for the peace that can flood their souls, making them the envy of others who see their obvious blessing.

This was to be the ultimate outcome in the persecution of the early Christians. Their witness was such that through their mended nets many souls were caught and brought to the kingdom of God.

The second blessing in 1 Peter 5:10 is "stablish." The idea here is to make you firm and solid. Muscles which had once been flabby and useless develop a firmness and solidity which turns a weakling into a person with special powers of resistance.

The third word is "strengthen"—to fill you with strength. The muscles which are made firm are now capable of being used to good effect. The added thought is that flabby fat is trimmed away, and the resultant person is capable of using the mended net with the firm and solid muscles in the body full of strength.

The last promise is to "settle you"—to anchor you, to lay a good foundation beneath you. The idea of the anchor is so valuable. If I am anchored to the rock, no matter how the storms may blow or the waves may beat and buffet I have a sure confidence. Nothing can shake me or move me from my blessed assurance in Christ.

This then is the second way in which the Lord Jesus can heal the brokenhearted. He heals for a purpose as I get involved with the God of all grace. He heals as he mends and as I follow him.

A Prayer for the Brokenhearted

My Father, I see myself in this message. Along with my broken heart are my broken nets. My hurt has taken up all my attention. I am only concerned with me.

Lord Jesus fill my soul with your presence and your power. Mend my nets, restore my weakened muscles, fill me with your strength, and let me feel the solid rock beneath my feet.

Anchor me to that rock with the assurance of faith, so I may be healed for a purpose, to be involved with Jesus Christ, the same yesterday, and today, and forever.

6.
For the Bound

The third group to whom our Lord promised blessing were those in bondage, "To preach deliverance to the captives" (Luke 4:18).

The more I travel and counsel with believers the more I realize how many confused, fearful people there are. The same story is repeated at every place I speak. On Sunday the church is full of pleasant people, well-dressed, and seemingly well-satisfied with life. But as the week goes by, and the message of the fullness of Christ is proclaimed, many come with their hurts, their fears, and their sheer inability to cope with life.

They are believers, saved, baptized, church members, even holding offices in the church, but there is a gray dullness about their daily experience. They have done all that they have been instructed to do, have fulfilled all the prerequisites, and yet the freedom, the deep joy, is missing in their daily lives.

In speaking with them I have found, in many cases, that the reason for their problems, when they open up their lives, is a deep-rooted sense of bondage. The "prison cell" may be a most expensive home, exquisitely furnished, and provided with every possible comfort and convenience; the "chains" may be of gold, even studded with diamonds; but the ultimate result is the same, a sense of bondage!

I want to tell you about two of the most common areas in which believers face fear and restriction. It is very possible that the words I am about to write will be just what the Lord wants you to hear. This is ever so when I preach the Word. Somehow the Lord brings in the very people who need to hear a certain message. Time and again people will come to me after a meeting, and each one will make the same comment, "That message was just for me!" May this be so in the reading of this chapter.

First then let us consider those who are in bondage to past sin and guilt. This is one of Satan's most powerful means of neutralizing the power of Christ in the daily life of a Christian.

Because of our decadent society, many people today are coming into the family of God with a lurid past. The rebellious extravagances of the sixties have produced a generation of adults and young marrieds who have tasted every sin in the book, whose minds were utterly corrupt, and whose bodies even today bear the resultant damage of their wild living.

I am meeting them as I counsel with them. Outwardly they have "covered over the cracks." They are truly saved, and they can "speak the language of Canaan"; but all the time there is a deep sense of their evil past. They can accept the fact of "respectable sins" being forgiven, but some of the things they have done are loathsome and utterly repugnant to their present standards.

It is an unusual experience to hear women discussing their past sinful connections, to hear men talking of gross sexual sins, to become aware of areas of corruption far below and beyond the "normal" level of sin.

These people have the assurance that God does forgive their ordinary sins, but what about those horrible things of the past?

It is possible to have a tiny sore on one's body which, if it is continually "picked," will spread and produce something of serious proportions. It is sometimes so with even a "small" sin. Satan can so encourage the "picking" of this "small" sin that it is blown up out of all proportion. So there can be a bondage to something which initially was of minor importance, but, as the mind focuses on the one spot repeatedly, the tiny threads of bondage wind around long enough to complete the captivity again and again.

To all such captives, whether the chains are iron, or gold, or just a simple thread wound around enough to paralyze, let me show you the glorious truth of words you already know.

In 1 John 1:8-9 we read: "If we say that we have no sin, we deceive ourselves, and the truth is not in us. If we confess our sins, he is faithful and just to forgive us our sins, and to cleanse us from all unrighteousness."

The words that impress me first of all are those five "If we" phrases in the chapter. I could have understood it easier if the apostle John had written "If you." If, when writing at the age of ninety plus, he had spoken ex cathedra to the lowly creatures of earth, excluding himself from the condemnation, I would have agreed immediately. But to read about the blessed apostle including himself in the sin situation is deeply moving to my soul.

Verse 9 is a truth to break all the chains of all the sins of every degree for all time in every human life! This includes you, whoever you may be, wherever you may be, in prison, or pew, or pulpit.

We are here distinctly taught that if we do one thing, then God will do two things in return.

The one thing we have to do is to confess our sins—not apologize for them or rationalize them, but drag them out into the open before the presence of a Holy God. If we will do this one thing, then the Lord will do two things. First, he will forgive us. Then he will cleanse us. He will forgive us because he is faithful. He will cleanse us because he is just.

He forgives us in heaven, and when he forgives, he forgets. There is thus no record in heaven of our sins—whatever they were. Chapter 2 underlines this fact in the first two verses: "My little children, these things write I unto you, that ye sin not. And if any man sin, we have an advocate with the Father, Jesus Christ the righteous: And he is the propitiation for our sins: and not for ours only, but also for the sins of the whole world."

This gracious offer of complete forgiveness is not an invitation to go further and deeper into sin, but a challenge to curb the life-style because of him who provides the cleansing.

Make sure you understand the mechanics of this forgiveness. Satan is called the accuser of the brethren (Rev. 12:10), but the Lord Jesus is here designated as our advocate. In Scotland today, if you were to appear on a charge before a judge you would seek the help of an *advocate*—the same word. We would use the word *lawyer* or *attorney*, someone who stands up for you, defends you, pleads your case.

The idea is that if Satan were to accuse you before Holy God, the Lord Jesus is there to defend you. The accusation leveled at you may be true—there may be many sins, evil deeds laid to your charge, but your Advocate is the propitiation for your sins. That means he is "the mercy seat"—the same word that was used concerning the ark in the holy of holies, where the high priest sprinkled the blood once a year on the Day of Atonement.

In other words, if Satan were to accuse you before the throne, the Lord Jesus is there on your behalf. He will point to his own shed blood and say: "I died for that sin; My precious blood was spilled for that sin." Because of the advocacy of our Lord our home in heaven is guaranteed. Satan may rightly say you are not worthy to enter because of the foulness of your evil past—and it would all be true, terribly true. But: "If we confess our sins, he is faithful and just to forgive" (1 John 1:9a).

The risen, victorious Christ seated at the right hand of the Father is the one who is the perfect assurance of your forgiveness and your home in heaven.

It would be blessing beyond compare even if that was all that was mine through acknowledging and confessing my sin, but that is only half of the truth. Verse 9 goes on to say: "and to cleanse us from all unrighteousness."

The reasoning is so beautifully simple. God is not only faithful to forgive in heaven, he is just here on earth. If there is no record in heaven of our sins, however grievous they may be, then there has to be no record of them here on earth. And so a just God cleanses you from all unrighteousness. See the same truth in verse 7: "The blood of Jesus Christ his Son cleanseth us from all sin." Notice it does not say "cleanseth us from all sin except. . . ." It is "from all sin"—period.

There is no record in heaven, and when God looks upon you he sees you spotless, accepted in the Beloved. Always remember that the word *justified* does not mean "just-as-if-I'd never sinned." It means that first I am cleansed of all my sin and guilt and then I am clothed in the righteousness of Christ.

But, you say, "How about my sin and guilt?" It is all gone! "But how about those horrible evil things I did?" They are all forgiven and you yourself in God's sight are clean from every stain.

"Then," you ask, "why am I in bondage? Why do I keep on remembering and recalling those evil things?"

One reason you recall them is because Satan hopes to neutralize you and to keep you in suspense, so he keeps on bringing them back to your mind.

Remember the story told of Martin Luther. It is said that one day the devil came and confronted him with part of his guilty past.

"Did you do these things, Martin Luther?"

"Yes," replied Luther.

"And do you think such a person is worthy to serve a Holy God?" demanded the devil.

"Is that all?" asked Luther.

"No," roared the devil. And he proceeded to read further sins from a long list in his hands.

"Did you do those?"

"Yes. Is that all?"

This continued until the enemy had recited all the listed sins of Martin Luther.

"There," cried the devil, "that is all. Now do you consider yourself fit to be a servant of a Holy God?"

"Master Devil," Luther replied, "take your pen and write across the whole list, "the blood of Jesus Christ his Son cleanses [me] from all sin."

If you are in bondage to your past sin and guilt, you must take your stand also. Claim what is yours. You do not deserve it. You have never earned it, nor are you worthy of such wonderful mercy. It is all of grace. Thank God for all that is yours in Christ. If the enemy keeps on recalling them to your mind, learn to say: "Thank you, Lord Jesus, that all is forgiven in your precious blood, and I am cleansed by a Holy God."

There are some people who agree with all we have just considered, and then they say, "Oh yes, I know God has forgiven me, but I can't forgive myself!"

This is supposed to be a demonstration of deep humility. Actually it is a demonstration of sheer pride, devilish pride! Such persons are implying that although Jesus shed his blood to procure forgiveness from a Holy God, it is not good enough to procure their own forgiveness of themselves. The whole idea is blasphemous. Don't ever let the devil put such thoughts into your mind.

The second great area of bondage in Christian living is being in bondage to present self and habits. This is so with many of God's people. They have a life-style to which they are bound as with fetters. Years of living under the influence of their fallen human nature has them firmly in the grip of old habits and thought patterns. They have struggled to get free from the bondage of the old behavior pattern but with little success. They know what they do is wrong; they long to have a different life; but somehow they never make it. There may be times when improvement seems in sight, but all too soon they slip back into the old ways. This is a fearful bondage, because we usually end by giving up the struggle for the right. Then we proceed to accept defeat as normal. Always remember, God did not save you to be just a failure!

We can find the answer to this problem in Romans 6:1-14. The very first verse sets the stage for the whole discussion: "Shall we continue in sin, that grace may abound?" Shall I just continue with my old habits and life-style, and trust Jesus to get me out of the mess? No wonder the second verse almost shouts out the answer: "God forbid. How shall we, that are dead to sin, live any longer therein?"

The chapter then proceeds to teach what I call the three "R's" of how to live the Christian life. This may be the very technique you have been seeking.

The first "R" I call *realize*. By that I mean realize that, in God's sight, when Christ died on the cross, I died also. The important phrase there is—"in God's sight." God has finished with fallen human nature. "So then they that are in the flesh cannot please God" (Rom. 8:8).

See how God has finished with human nature in these following verses: "We were baptized into his death" (v. 3); "We are buried with him by baptism into death" (v. 4); "We have been planted together in the likeness of his death" (v. 5); "Our old man [the old nature] is crucified with him" (v. 6); "Now if we be dead with Christ" (v. 8).

This is called the identification of the believer with Christ in his death. Notice the repeated idea—with him—planted together—with him.

I remember when I was first saved I was full of love for the Lord. I wanted to serve him. I wanted my life to count for him. I was all set on living for Jesus. In doing so, I missed the whole point of the first "R." You also may be struggling to beat your old life-style into shape, to make it acceptable to God. The devil will encourage you to do this because as soon as you start on this adventure you are in bondage. You are trying to do the impossible and the unrequested. It sounds so noble, just the natural thing to do. This is exactly what it is—the natural thing to do. But when we become believers we are lifted out of the natural into the supernatural. Colossians 1:13 says: "Who hath delivered us from the power of darkness, and hath translated us into the kingdom of his dear Son."

Second Corinthians 5:17-18 tells us: "Therefore if any man be in Christ, he is a new creature: old things are passed away; behold, all things are become new. And all things are of God."

We get so busy trying to improve our old behavior pattern, trying to get rid of the bad things, and to work hard at improving any so-called "good" things. And all the time the correct way is to realize that, in God's sight, when Christ died, I died. I have to learn to count myself out of this Christian life ethic.

God does not want me to live for Jesus, but to die for him! Paul had the right idea in Galatians 2:20: "I am crucified with Christ: nevertheless I live: yet not I, but Christ liveth in me!" Notice the same phrase again "with Christ."

The second "R" helps us to understand the method a little better. Romans 6:11 says: "Likewise reckon ye also yourselves to be dead indeed unto sin, but alive unto God through Jesus Christ our Lord." There is the second "R" *reckon*—this means "act as if it were so." The first word was *realize*—that in God's sight when Christ died, I died. That is true in God's sight, but in my own sight and my daily experience "I" am very much alive. "I" is my fallen human nature, my "heart," my personality. "I" am, in fact, my greatest enemy. I am in bondage to my fallen human nature as we saw before, the old behavior pattern of habits and thought patterns.

But if I can accept God's Word and realize that God has finished with fallen human nature and then realize in a new and wonderful way that God has sent his Son to indwell me, then I am on the way to blessing.

If I go on to reckon myself out of the situations, confrontations, and decisions, and allow the indwelling Christ to take over, then I am further on the way to blessing.

The third "R" is *respond*. The word in the Bible is "yield." Romans 6:13 says: "Neither yield ye your members as instruments of unrighteousness unto sin: but yield yourselves unto God, . . . and your members as instruments of righteousness unto God."

The whole process becomes a simple progression of involvement with the Lord. *I realize* God has finished with human nature—that is why he gave us a new nature—"that by these ye might be partakers of the divine nature" (2 Pet. 1:4). Christ himself is indwelling each believer in all his risen Power.

Then *I reckon* myself out of the issues of life, and *I respond* by yielding my members to the Lord. The term "my members" means all that I possess—my body, my skills, my strength, my abilities—is yielded to God. The reason for yielding all is so that they can be "instruments" in the hand of God. The word *instrument* means a tool, a weapon, an implement.

Thus all I possess is in the hand of God to do with as he will.

In this way the bondage of the old behavior pattern is broken as I yield my life, not to my own choices, but unreservedly to God.

Do not miss the lovely thought of the believer as a tool in the hand of God, or a weapon, or an implement. A tool is to work with, a weapon is to fight with, an implement is for construction—each representing the various ways in which the Lord can take and use the yielded life.

Thinking collectively, a church fellowship is, in a sense, God's tool kit in that place—different tools for differing jobs. Tools need to be clean and sharp. So it is with the believer.

This which we have just considered is not just a bright idea, or an alternative way of life. It is the way. There is no other way. Jesus said, "I am the way, the truth, and the life" (John 14:6).

If I refuse to realize, to reckon, to respond, then I am deliberately going against the will of God. In doing so I am condemning myself to the bondage of failure and denying the Lord the life for which he died.

I speak from years of experience, from being on both sides of the fence. There is no joy in all this world to compare with the wonder of the truth, "He hath anointed me . . . to preach deliverance to the captives." To see myself, day by day, in the hands of the Lord, that his will might be done in me and through me, all this brings the peace of God which passes all understanding. And all this is available to you if you only realize, reckon, and respond.

A Prayer for Those in Bondage

Heavenly Father, this is beginning to make sense to me at last. No wonder I am in bondage to the past when I keep on remembering what you have forgiven and forgotten.

No wonder I am in bondage to the present when I try to improve what you have finished with.

Dear God, set me free both from the past and from the present.

Teach me day by day to realize, reckon, and respond. Then I, too, can say: "For me to live is Christ" (Phil. 1:21).

May it be so for your greater glory.

7.
For the Blind

As our Lord read those blessed words that sabbath morning in Nazareth (Luke 4:18-21), he spoke of a fourth group. He said he was anointed to bring "recovering of sight to the blind" (v. 18). His own comment was, "This day is this scripture fulfilled in your ears" (v. 21).

We have been learning how vital is that ministry of the Lord today, and day by day—first to the bankrupt, then the brokenhearted, then to those in bondage, and now to the blind.

This has much to say to us, especially when we notice the words "recovering of sight." This is not a first-time giving, but a recovering of that which has somehow been lost.

How true this is of many believers today. Once they could see. Their eyes had been opened to the blessings of God and their vision was set on his ways, but now all that was theirs is gone.

This could be true of you who are reading these words. Were you once alert and alive for Jesus? But has the fire now gone, just the dullness of ashes remaining? Have you lost your vision? Are your eyes blinded to the will and the way of the Lord?

How good to know that our Lord was anointed to bring recovering of sight to such as you. What is more, he says: "This day is this scripture fulfilled in your ears." As you attend to his teaching in this chapter, this could be your day to recover that which you once had, to go on to see greater things.

I want to turn your attention to John 9:1-38. This is the story of the man who was blind from his birth. There are too many verses to quote here, but it would be a good help to you if you had the chapter open before you. After all, we are discussing the use of eyes!

The story of this man is an excellent study in a continuing relationship with Jesus. This can be seen in the progression of terminology he used when describing our Lord.

In verse 11 he referred to the Lord as "A man that is called Jesus." In verse 17, replying to the Pharisees, he said, "He is a prophet." The Pharisees said, "We know that God spake unto Moses: as for this fellow, we know not from whence he is" (v. 29).

The beggar answered them by affirming, "If this man were not of God, he could do nothing" (v. 33).

Further on in the chapter the Lord met him and said, "Dost thou believe on the Son of God?" (v. 35). To this the beggar gave the glorious answer, "Lord, I believe" (v. 38).

What a tremendous appreciation this beggar showed—all because his eyes were opened to see.

The most important thing in this chapter is to realize that the man had two meetings with Jesus. The first occasion was when he was sightless, but even so he believed what Jesus told him. He proved his belief by responding to the direction of the Lord: "He went his way therefore, and washed, and came seeing" (v. 7).

On this first occasion he "believed to see."

The second meeting was when the Lord came to him after he had been cast out of the synagogue. This time the man had eyes that could see, but he did not recognize the Lord. He had never seen Jesus before.

Then followed that amazing dialogue: "Dost thou believe on the Son of God? He answered and said, Who is he, Lord, that I might believe on him? And Jesus said unto him, Thou has both seen him, and it is he that talketh with thee. And he said, Lord, I believe. And he worshipped him" (vv. 35-38).

On the first meeting the beggar "believed to see." On the second meeting "he saw to believe!"

It was this second meeting that produced the act of worship as he came face to face with the Son of God.

With this story and this experience before us, turn now to 1 John 4 and see something which many people have never realized. This section is teaching that it is possible today to have two meetings with the Lord, each with amazing results.

"In this was manifested the love of God toward us, because that God sent his only begotten Son into the world, that we might live through him. Herein is love, not that we loved God, but that he loved us, and sent his Son to be the propitiation for our sins" (vv. 9-10).

In each verse it is recorded that God sent his Son. There are two sendings. That is why it is possible to have two meetings.

When I first started to read John's Epistles I thought there was a lot of repetition. It seemed to me that John was saying the same thing in several different ways, and I found it confusing. But as the Lord has led me on in his Word I have found quite a different picture.

For example, the two verses quoted above seemed once to be identical, each about God sending his Son. But when we examine each verse a tremendous truth emerges.

Look at verse 10. We are told that God sent his son to be the propitiation for our sins. We saw the word *propitiation* in chapter 6 of this book when we were considering the forgiveness of sins. There we saw that God was faithful to forgive, and just to cleanse us from all sin, on the basis of the death of Christ and his shed blood. The word *propitiation* means the mercy seat where the blood was shed.

We thus find that the sending of the Son in verse 10 was in connection with his death, how he saved us when he died for us on the cross—his saving death. But verse 9 tells us something very different. Notice who was sent: "God sent his only begotten Son." The phrase "only begotten son" has a special significance in the Bible.

Come with me as we find the mystery of the "only begotten Son." Look first in Psalm 2, that great messianic psalm which speaks of the Lord Jesus. See in verses 6 and 7: "Yet have I set my king upon my holy hill of Zion. I will declare the decree: the Lord hath said unto me, Thou art my Son; this day have I begotten thee." There is the same word again: "This day have I begotten thee." Obviously, this is referring to the Lord Jesus, but the question is, "What day was he begotten?"

Look now again in Acts 13, which we have already considered in chapter 3, and see the great sermon Paul preached in Antioch. Notice in verse 16 to whom he was speaking: "Then Paul stood up, and beckoning with his hand said, Men of Israel, and ye that fear God, give audience." He was speaking not only to the Jews but also to the Gentiles—to whoever feared God.

In verses 28 and 29 he spoke of the crucifixion of our Lord. In verse 30 he declared: "But God raised him from the dead."

Then comes, in verses 32 and 33, a tremendous truth so often overlooked by believers: "And we declare unto you glad tidings, how that the promise which was made unto the fathers, God hath fulfilled the same unto us their children, in that he hath raised up Jesus again."

Before we finish verses 32 and 33, pause a moment to see part of that great truth: "The promise . . . God hath fulfilled the same . . . in that he hath raised up Jesus again." Notice very carefully that the promise of salvation was fulfilled in the resurrection.

This may seem just a matter of words to some people, but the whole secret of the success of the early church is seen here. The promise of salvation was not fulfilled at the cross. It was implemented at the cross, but it was fulfilled in the resurrection.

Wherever the gospel was preached in early church times, the climax of the message was always the same. They offered to men and women the risen, victorious Christ to indwell them by his Holy Spirit.

Much of evangelism today centers on the cross, offering to men and women a dying Savior who can deal with the whole question of their sin. Thank God that the cross is proclaimed. But if the message ends at the cross, the whole message has not been told. The promise of salvation was fulfilled in the resurrection!

It is possible to preach the cross and not to mention the resurrection, but you cannot preach the resurrection without mentioning the cross.

Look again at verse 33: "God hath fulfilled the same unto us their children, in that he hath raised up Jesus again, as it is also written in the second psalm, Thou art my Son, this day have I begotten thee."

Now see set forth so clearly which day this was. This Scripture speaks of the raising of Jesus from the dead. Thus the "begotten Son" is the risen Christ.

Now take this great truth and place it in the context of 1 John 4:9: "God sent his only begotten Son into the world, that we might live through him." This is telling us of the sending of Jesus, the risen, victorious Christ, into our hearts that we might live through him.

When we now compare the two verses in 1 John 4 it is obvious that the two sendings are quite different. Verse 10 speaks of Jesus dying for us. Verse 9 speaks of Jesus living for us.

Every believer has had the first look at Christ, the first sending when he came to save us from our sins. But not every believer has had the second look, has seen him in the second sending, when he comes to live in us, for us, and through us.

This could be your problem. Perhaps you have only seen him once. Thank God for that first look whereby your sins are forgiven and you have a home in heaven. But that isn't enough. That isn't all.

Jesus said in Luke 4 that he was sent to bring recovering of sight to the blind. How wonderful it would be if you could recover the initial joy and vision you had when you first met him.

There is no need to try to live for him, to struggle to make the grade. Verse 9 says "that we might live through him"—not for him, but through him.

Some of God's people do not "live," they just exist from one crisis to the next.

That is not God's plan for us. Paul could say: "For me to live is Christ" (Phil. 1:21). "I can do all things through Christ" (Phil. 4:13). Paul proved it to be true. God has no favorites. He never gave Paul any more than he is willing to give you—the indwelling victorious Christ.

The great need now is so to yield day by day to the power and plan of Christ that day by day we learn to live through him. This is no sudden, super change but the gradual outworking of his life through me as day by day I allow him to live in me and through me. In this way I meet him the second time.

At first, like the beggar in John 9, we believe to see. Our sins are forgiven; we have a home in heaven.

Then we meet him in all his risen power, and we see to believe—to believe that he indwells us, that as we recognize his lordship and allow him to use us as the tools we read of in Romans 6. Then we really start to live through him.

How many looks have you had?

A Prayer for a Blind Believer

Dear Father, this is so challenging. I can see myself again in this story.

I have seen you, Lord Jesus, on the cross. I have believed you died for me.

FOR THE BLIND

But now, Lord, I want to see you as the risen, victorious Christ indwelling me, never to leave me.
Lord Jesus show me how all this can come true in my life.
"Open my eyes that I may see,
Glimpses of truth thou hast for me!"[1]
Let me learn to worship, like the beggar, "Lord, I believe!"

Note

1. Clara H. Scott, "Open My Eyes that I May See," *Baptist Hymnal* 1975, p. 358.

8.
For the Bruised

When we review the five groups mentioned in Luke 4:18, we can see a progression in heartache and suffering, until we come to the last group. The brokenhearted are worse off than the bankrupt. Those in bondage are one stage worse than the brokenhearted. The blind are surely more stricken than the bound. But when we look at the last group, "the bruised," the downward tendency appears to have stopped.

After all, being bruised is nothing very serious. This is an everyday experience to some of us.

But when we stop and look for the original word which is here translated "bruised," we find something totally different. In no way does the original word mean just a simple bruising. The actual meaning is "broken in pieces," totally smashed, with no hope of being restored to the original condition. With this in mind we now see that the fifth group is the worst—the end of the line. These are the hopeless cases.

There were new resources for the bankrupt, healing for the brokenhearted, deliverance for the bound, and recovery of sight for the blind, but how about these broken people? The Lord promised "to set at liberty them that are bruised."

This chapter tells of the ultimate in human suffering and of God's answer to that which cannot be healed or restored. In one sense it tells what to do when divine healing is not granted. Always remember that divine healing is a sovereign act of God, very often inexplicable as to why it is given or not given. Also, realize the obvious— there has to be divine nonhealing, or people would never die. Even the greatest "faith healers" have a deathbed experience!

The Lord Jesus said he would "set at liberty" those who were crushed and broken. He would set them free in the midst of their

FOR THE BRUISED

brokenness. They would learn to live with it, to live in it, and to live out of it. This is truly the ultimate in human experience.

We can learn a great deal concerning this if we compare the record of 2 Corinthians 11:23-33 with that of 2 Corinthians 12:1-10.

In chapter 11, Paul is replying to some of the remarks made to him by the Christians in Corinth. They had been telling Paul about the preachers they had heard recently. These men had tremendous stories to tell of themselves. They had left a great impression of how important they were because of what they had experienced for God.

Because of this Paul was led to do what he seldom did, to speak of himself and what he had suffered for Christ. We can be glad that the Corinthians showed such poor taste. Otherwise we would never have had this information concerning Paul and his suffering.

"Are they ministers of Christ? (I speak as a fool) I am more; in labours more abundant, in stripes above measure, in prisons more frequent, in deaths oft. Of the Jews five times received I forty stripes save one. Thrice was I beaten with rods, once was I stoned, thrice I suffered shipwreck, a night and a day I have been in the deep" (2 Cor. 11:23-25).

It comes as a surprise to many people when they begin to understand the details of Paul's sufferings, as listed here.

When the Romans conquered a nation they allowed the people to retain much of their freedom—as compared with the behavior of previous world powers. This was one of the reasons for the success of the Roman Empire.

Certain things were always denied the conquered people. One was the right to inflict the death penalty. That is why the Jews had to come to Pilate and request permission to execute the Lord Jesus.

Did you ever consider that section of miraculous prophecy? Psalm 22 is a detailed description of the Roman method of crucifixion. Yet when David wrote those words the Roman Empire had not even begun. It was an unknown, future entity.

The method of execution for blasphemy, as set forth in the Old Testament, was stoning. But for the presence of Pilate, the Lord Jesus would have been stoned to death, as was Stephen in Acts 7:59. Yet every word of Psalm 22 came true on that first Good Friday. The Scriptures were fullfilled to the letter. This was indeed a miracle of foretelling.

The ultimate punishment allowed to the Jews was "forty stripes save one"—thirty-nine multiple lashes.

This was a most vicious, sadistic method of causing pain and suffering. The victims were stripped and tied spread-eagled to the execution apparatus. The executioner stood by with a short handled whip which contained several long leather thongs, each of which had metal or bone inserts at regular intervals. There was someone to count the thirty-nine lashes. There were buckets of water to throw over the victim if he fainted. Each lash had to be consciously experienced.

And so the lashes were administered. Each stroke sent the long thongs wrapping around the naked body. As they were dragged free, the flesh was torn and ripped. Sometimes the victim was blinded as the metal punctured the unprotected eyes. Sometimes the victim died under the intensity of the violence.

It does not take a vivid imagination to see that when a man had received the full quota of stripes he would be a bloody mass of quivering humanity, marked and scarred for life.

Now with this in mind read verse 24 again. "Of the Jews five times received I forty stripes save one." The horror of it—not just once did Paul suffer such awful torture, but five times! A total of 195 lashes ripped and tore into his defenseless body. Even the thought of the thing is ghastly.

But that was not all. In the next verse he tells that three times he was beaten with rods. In this form of punishment, a torturer with a handful of rods beat the back of his victim as long as he felt necessary. You who suffer from back or disc trouble, just consider what such violence would do to the backbone, especially if there had been the previous experience of the thirty-nine lashes administered five times.

Verse 25 must be the extreme in understatement. Three experiences are lumped together in the one verse. First the beatings, then the stoning, then the shipwrecks.

We have more details of the stoning in Acts 14:19-20. Did you ever see the miracle that is hidden in those two verses? "And having stoned Paul, they drew him out of the city, supposing he had been dead" (Acts 14:19). When they were sure he was dead, they dragged his body out of the city to dump it on the garbage pit where the dogs and the vultures did a marvelous job of disposing of any edible object.

"Howbeit, as the disciples stood round about him, he rose up, and came into the city: and the next day he departed with Barnabas to Derbe" (Acts 14:20).

Here is the miracle—Paul, who was presumed to be dead, rose up, returned to the city of Lystra and the next day he set out to walk the sixty miles to Derbe. Most of us could not walk sixty miles at the best of times, but here the miraculous happened in the experience of Paul.

The third item listed in verse 25 is "Thrice I suffered shipwreck, a night and a day I have been in the deep."

This reveals something we never knew before. We have just one account of Paul in a shipwreck, in Acts 27. But here he tells us he was shipwrecked three times, and on one occasion he was over thirty-six hours adrift in the open sea. And so Paul continued his record of suffering and sorrow to vindicate himself in the eyes of the immature Corinthian Christians.

Now the whole point of recounting this is to show that he was delivered out of all his trials. All his wounds healed. All the broken limbs were mended. Only the scars remained.

But when we come to chapter 12 we are dealing with a totally different situation. Paul began by telling of certain mysterious experiences he had: "Whether in the body, . . . or out of the body, I cannot tell; God knoweth" (vv. 2-3). He speaks of a visit to "the third heaven," and then to "paradise" where he "heard unspeakable words, which it is not lawful" to repeat.

Then he continues, "And lest I should be exalted above measure through the abundance of the revelations, there was given to me a thorn in the flesh, the messenger of Satan to buffet me, lest I should be exalted above measure. For this thing I besought the Lord thrice, that it might depart from me" (vv. 7-8).

Many commentators have tried to elucidate what "the thorn" really was, blindness, leprosy, a hunchback, or other possible areas of weakness. But, the truth is, the Bible does not tell us. If we knew exactly what "the thorn" really was, then perhaps only those people suffering from a similar complaint could claim a measure of help. As it is, no one knows, so everyone can be encouraged.

One thing we do know is this. There are two distinct words in the original, each of which is translated by the one word *thorn*. One word is *acanthus* which describes the thorns on shrubs, bushes, and trees, the crown of thorns, and other similar vegetable products. That is the most common word used.

The other word is *skolops*, which is used only once in the Bible—in this reference. It has nothing at all to do with thorns, as we normally think of them. The actual meaning is a sharp, pointed wooden stake, such as is used for supporting young trees in the garden. This was "the thorn" that gave Paul all that distress and agony, something which seemed to pierce him through and through, something which was visible in front and at the rear, something which gave excruciating pain. It was for this awful agony that he cried out three times to God, begging for relief and release.

It is obvious why he would beseech God to deliver him. The experience was so limiting, making it so hard for him to keep up the pace. If only he were strong again the better he would be as a servant of God. Humanly speaking, common sense demanded a healing. Otherwise, all the missionary work and outreach would suffer.

But he was never healed! Some people say if you are not healed it proves you did not have enough faith. Who had more faith than Paul? Did he deserve to be healed? Was he worthy? Yes, if any one deserved to be so blessed, Paul was that man. And, yet, he was never healed.

Instead, God gave him an answer which is the final answer to all unanswerable suffering. It is the answer which explains the words of Christ in Luke 4:18. He was going to set at liberty those who were broken and crushed so that they could learn to live with it, to live in it, and to live out of it!

Here then is that divine answer: "My grace is sufficient for thee: for my strength is made perfect in weakness" (v. 9).

God said to Paul, "You are more use to me with the thorn. It gives me an opportunity to demonstrate my power."

Notice that the thorn did not hinder God's full purpose. The thorn was itself part of God's plan and purpose.

Paul could now do one of two things. This choice always comes to the believer when faced with such an impossible situation. He can resist and fight the whole situation, saying it is not fair, or asking why God should do this to him?

This is the way many believers react today. They cannot understand the situation. They cry to God for help. God does not hear them. So, they think, *What's the use?* They fall out with God and proceed to blame him for his unkindness. In doing so, they condemn themselves to increasing deadness and hopelessness.

Paul did the other thing. He accepted the situation, believing the Lord knew what he was doing and trusting him to work it out his way. "Most gladly therefore will I rather glory in my infirmities, that the power of Christ may rest upon me. Therefore I take pleasure in infirmities, in reproaches, in necessities, in persecutions, in distresses for Christ's sake: for when I am weak, then am I strong" (vv. 9-10).

Paul was a perfect example of "them that are bruised" as mentioned in Luke 4:18. He was truly "broken in pieces," totally smashed, with no hope of restoration. But the Lord set him at liberty. He found pleasure in his brokenness. The power of Christ rested on him. When he was weak, then, especially then, was he strong. He learned to live in, and through, and out of his tragedy. In doing so, he gave glory to God and gladness to himself.

Remember, once more, God has no favorites. He never gave Paul any more than he gives you or me.

The thing that counts most in daily living is not how much you possess, but what you do with what you have. It is not how much you know, but what you do with what you know.

So many of us have an increasing amount of "knowing" but a decreasing amount of "doing."

We have thus dealt with all five groups. We have seen "Jesus Today" as God's answer for the hurts and sorrows that beset many of the Lord's people.

Luke 4:19 gives the final words that Jesus read that sabbath morning: "To preach the acceptable year of the Lord."

The final question is, "What are you going to do with such a glorious offer of blessing?"

You can either accept, and get involved with the risen life of Christ, as he indwells you day by day, or you can push to one side his goodness and treat it as unacceptable. Why not give him the opportunity to prove himself, "Jesus Today," as the one answer to your every need?

A Prayer for the Bruised

Thank you, Heavenly Father, for sending Jesus to be the answer to the needs of the bankrupt, the brokenhearted, the bound, the blind, and the bruised.

I come with all my need and emptiness. Help me more and more to accept what I cannot understand and to trust you with all my future. I believe what you have just taught me. I believe Jesus indwells me, never to leave me. I believe he will be to me all that I will ever need. Thank you, Jesus.

PART II
WHAT HE ASKS

9.
"What Seek Ye?"

There have been many remarkable changes in human behavior patterns during this last generation. There was a time when we spoke about "the silent masses," when children were "seen and not heard," and the majority of society went on their way accepting things and conditions as they were. Sometimes it was a sullen silence, but generally it was quietly unresponsive.

All that has now disappeared. The silence has given way to growing demands to be heard. The world is full of questions with often not much interest in the answers given. The invasion of radio and TV have altered the old adage. Now children are "**heard** and not seen!" Our world has turned from the punctuation marks of period and comma to those of question and exclamation.

Thinking of the questions people ask today caused me to search the Scriptures and explore some of the questions that were asked by our Lord. I have found this to be a fascinating study, for many reasons.

John 2:25 says, "He knew what was in man." No one had to tell him what people were thinking.

In Mark 2:8 he said, "Why reason ye these things in your hearts?" And in Matthew 9:4, "Jesus knowing their thoughts said, Wherefore think ye evil in your hearts?"

He never had to ask the questions to obtain information. He knew already. He asked not to discover, but to lead the persons to whom he was speaking to discover for themselves. He put people on the spot. He forced them to make decisions. He let them hear themselves speaking. This is one of the major objectives in counseling today.

It is with this in view that I begin Part II of this book. I want to take some of these seemingly simple questions that Jesus asked and let them do a deep work in all of our hearts.

Maybe he will put us on the spot, lead us to make decisions and, in so doing, discover our real selves, and our true attitudes and values.

The first question I want us to consider is found in John's Gospel, chapter 1. It concerns two disciples of John the Baptist.

These young men were not professional religious leaders but simple fishermen looking for answers to living. They had heard the dynamic preaching of John and had responded to his challenge. John's great cry was, "Repent—bring forth fruits worthy of repentance" (AT). He was sent to prepare the way for our Lord.

These young men had thoroughly responded and repented, but, somehow, the act of repentance had not satisfied all their searching. Thus it was when they heard John speak of the person and work of Jesus they were more than just interested. They were looking for something more than the negative approach of John.

So we read in John 1:35-36, "Again the next day after John stood, and two of his disciples; And looking upon Jesus as he walked, he saith, Behold the Lamb of God!" They responded to John's words by following Jesus. It was then that the Lord asked his great question. "Then Jesus turned, and saw them following, and saith unto them, What seek ye?" (v. 38).

These are the first recorded words of our Lord as set forth in John's Gospel. It is interesting to see the other challenging words that follow in the same chapter. First, as we have seen, is the question. Then, in verse 39 is the invitation, "Come and see." Verse 43 presents the command, "Follow me."

Meditate for a moment on this divine sequence. See it as the way the Lord moves into your life—the question, the invitation, the command. The progression is so simple, but the purpose is so profound. I stop, look, and listen, and my whole life is revolutionized.

Consider for a moment the fact, seen above, that repentance and forgiveness alone did not satisfy the longing desires of these two young men. They were seeking for something more, and they found it in the person of the Lord Jesus.

This same fact is true in our response to the gospel today. If all I can find in the gospel is forgiveness of sins through repentance and the glorious hope of a home in heaven, I, too, will remain unsatisfied. Such a discovery gives me forgiveness for the past, and a bright hope for the future, but it leaves me on my own, facing the present tense of living with all its hurts and failures. Thank God for all the provision for the past and the future, but that alone cannot satisfy the aching hunger of the human heart.

Romans 5:8-10 tell us the complete story in all its sufficiency. Verse 8 tells me of a full forgiveness, "God commendeth his love toward us, in that, while we were yet sinners, Christ died for us." The past is dealt with once and for all, "One sacrifice for sins for ever" (Heb. 10:12).

Verse 9 spells out the glorious certainty for the future, "Much more then, being now justified by his blood, we shall be saved from wrath through him."

But verse 10 is one of the superlative verses of the Bible. It was this very verse which opened for me a door into a new life in the here and now, "For if, when we were enemies, we were reconciled to God by the death of his Son, much more, being reconciled, we shall be saved by his life."

Notice the buildup of the two words "much more." There is more than forgiveness of sins—much more—there is a home in heaven. Similarly, there is more than a home in heaven—much more—there is the experience of being saved by his life.

Just as these two young men were looking for something more in their salvation experience, so, today, many believers, are searching for something more. These young men found the answer in a relationship with Christ, day by day. And so it is with us today. What we need is not a new experience, but a new relationship with the risen Christ. We need to respond to his command, "Follow me!" In doing so we, too, can be daily delivered from sin's dominion—from the pressures of temptation, sin, guilt, sorrow, frustration, and the host of other attendant heartaches—delivered by his resurrection life, by his indwelling Holy Spirit. This can only come true as we experience that new relationship with the risen, victorious Christ, day by day.

But, let us come back to that first great question, "What seek ye?" In the privacy of these pages let me be personal and ask, what are you looking for in life?

Of course, it all depends upon your profession and the situation in which you find yourself now. But, even so, we can find one answer to cover all the many and varied responses to such a question. The one answer is "success."

Whatever your position in life, in thought or word or deed, your hopes and aspirations are all directed towards one goal—that you may have some measure of success in response to your efforts.

This fact we can all agree upon, but the most important part of this consideration is not the fact of success, but the meaning of the very word itself. What is success? What do we mean by success?

To many people this may seem a foolish question to ask. Why, everyone knows what success is. It is making a fortune, having a big home, enjoying life, being famous. Is this success? Is it really?

Ask the people who have made the fortune, who live in the big homes, those who are celebrities. In most cases they will not call such possessions success.

Our Western world has a simple definition for success. It is "bigger and better." Those of you who are in the business world know how true this is. So long as the sales' graph goes up and up, that is success. But, if it plateaus, be careful now, watch it! And, if the graph starts to go down, start looking for another job. Because success is "bigger and better," all else is failure!

As I meet and counsel with believers in all parts of this world, I find so many who are involved in this rat race for success. Some are excited; they are making the grade. Others are broken and defeated; they have failed.

There is only one answer to this turbulent issue of success or failure; it is to find out what success is in the eyes of God. Men's standards vacillate, but, "Jesus Christ" is "the same yesterday, and today, and for ever" (Heb. 13:8). God's standards are the same in the New Testament as they were in the Old Testament. God has only one definition of success. Here it is, Success is obedience to the known, revealed will of God, regardless of the consequences. The two key thoughts there are first, "obedience" and second, "regardless of the consequences."

We can all probably agree on the first word, "obedience." It is the second phrase which tests our lives, "whatever the consequences in my life!" We are apt to judge success by material results. We do the same thing in our churches. The successful pastor is the one with the large church, with the new building program, with the radio and TV outreach. He must be successful with such a program.

The challenging thing is to judge the ministry of Paul by such standards. Measure his imprisonments, his agonies over churches falling away, his eventual execution. The verdict is failure.

Better still, measure the ministry of the Lord himself by the results, so obvious. Twelve apostles were left at the end of three year's intensive ministry: one betrayed him; one denied him; the rest ran away. He was taken and crucified. The verdict of the world was failure.

And yet we know that that was not failure. It was the most glorious success of time and eternity. We ourselves are part of the ever outgoing fruit of his obedience.

Always remember the words of Isaiah 55:8, "For my thoughts are not your thoughts, neither are your ways my ways, saith the Lord." If we can only accept this truth and then seek God's thoughts and his ways, we will be in a position to take a second look at this word *success* and see it as God sees it, obedience to the known, revealed will of God, regardless of the consequences.

With this thought in mind look with me at the life story of Isaiah, one of the giants of the Old Testament. Here is a man whose success is unquestioned, whose book has been an inspiration down through the ages.

Look in chapter 6 where we read of his call to the ministry. It begins with his vision of the holiness of God. All true service for the Lord must be based on that vision, the holiness of God.

This concept of holiness is a much neglected truth in today's repertoire of teaching. The big emphasis is on the love of God. Thank the Lord for such an emphasis. But that is not the supreme attribute of God. The holiness of God is the central theme of the Word of God, the Bible. Calvary was necessary because of the holiness of God.

Look in Psalm 22 and compare verse 1 with verse 3, "My God, my God why hast thou forsaken me?" "But thou art holy."

Isaiah 6:3 emphasizes the same fact: "One cried unto another, and said Holy, holy, holy, is the Lord of hosts: the whole earth is full of his glory."

As we are considering Isaiah's call to a successful ministry, it is helpful to learn the lesson taught in verse 2, when we read of the ministry of the seraphim. "Each one had six wings; with twain he covered his face, and with twain he covered his feet, and with twain he did fly" (v. 2). Notice the order given, "his face, his feet, did fly." The covering of the face denotes *worship* to the holy God. The covering of the feet is telling of the *walk* before a holy God. The use of the wings in the third instance, flying, tells of the *work* for a holy God.

Here then is a simple demonstration by angelic beings of the divine order of emphasis in successful ministry. First comes my attitude of *worship* to a holy God. Then comes my own personal *walk* before that same holy God. The walk is the outcome of the worship. Finally, the *work* I do is a product based on my own life-style, which itself is dependent on my response to the holiness of God.

The important teaching is underlined by the response of Isaiah to the vision he saw of "the Lord sitting upon a throne, high and lifted up" (v. 1).

Verses 5 to 12 detail the sequence of events in the young man's life as a result of this vision. We see first his confession, then his cleansing, then his commission from the hands of Almighty God.

Isaiah at this time would be a young man full of love and obedience to God and resplendent in all the beauty of a pure life. But when he saw himself in the awful searching light of the holiness of God he cried, "Woe is me! for I am undone; because I am a man of unclean lips, and I dwell in the midst of a people of unclean lips: for mine eyes have seen the King, the Lord of hosts" (v. 5).

His response is typical of that of all the great saints of God down through the ages. Regardless of denomination, once they have drawn near and stood in the holy light of God's presence, their cry has been the same as the awfulness of sin has been revealed. The reason is simple; the closer we get to the light, the more it reveals. If I live in the fringe area of God's holiness I can maintain a life-style which is acceptable to my lowered standards. But once I draw nearer to the light, all that is sordid is revealed. If I dare to go into the inner presence, everything is seen. Even my "good" points stand out in all their selfish impurity.

Thus it was that from Isaiah's lips there poured out a confession of sin. Notice his reference to "unclean lips," both concerning himself and those among whom he dwelt.

The word used here in the Hebrew for "unclean" is the same word used in describing the effects of leprosy in Leviticus. The leper had to cry "unclean, unclean," and this is what Isaiah cried. He saw himself as a spiritual leper in the sight of a holy God.

The cleansing by the seraphim is described in verses 6 and 7. The live coal came from off the altar, and it was laid on those same unclean lips. The result was twofold. First, his iniquity was taken away. This referred to the perversity of his fallen human nature and the guilt associated with that inherent selfishness. Then his sin was purged; his hostile acts were forgiven. His iniquity was "what he was"; his sin was "what he did."

In New Testament language this is seen in 2 Corinthians 5:17, "Therefore if any man be in Christ, he is a new creature: old things are passed away; behold all things are become new. And all things are of God, who hath reconciled us to himself by Jesus Christ." This does not mean that we are sinlessly perfect but that we have a new relationship to a holy God as we are indwelt by his Holy Spirit.

With Isaiah it came through a live coal from off the altar. With us, it comes through the Lamb of God who was offered on that altar! One is the type. The other is the glorious fulfillment.

Now comes the third step on the pathway to a successful ministry. Having confessed himself and his sin, he is cleansed. Now the cleansed servant is ready to be commissioned. We read this in verses 8-9: "Also I heard the voice of the Lord, saying, Whom shall I send, and who will go for us? Then said I, Here am I, send me. And he said, go."

Notice in verse 8 the unity and the Trinity of God. "Whom shall I send, and who will go for us?" The word *Trinity* as such is not found in the Bible, but there are several Scriptures where the concept is taught. This is one of them. God called Isaiah, but it was the Trinity who sent him: Father, Son, and Holy Spirit.

When I was a young believer, I often heard messages based on this story. They always ended on a note of glory, "And he said, Go." I was left with the picture of this young man striding out into a life full of blessing and success. Isaiah's book was so amazing in its presentation of truth, I assumed his daily life would have been equally resplendent in glorious success.

But that was not to be. This is where this message of success, as God sees it, comes to its crisis. If we read on in verses 9 to 12, we come upon a remarkable situation. We find that the Lord was sending Isaiah, but he was also telling him what would happen as he served the Lord. Isaiah learned that no one would listen to his preaching, no one would respond to his ministry. He would pour out his heart and see no results. His life would be one of seemingly unfulfilled service.

To this Isaiah cries in verse 11, "Then said I, Lord, how long?" He wanted to know the worst, how long this condition was to continue. The answer he received was one of chilling finality—always!

Now just stop and consider the situation in which Isaiah found himself. He was cleansed and commissioned but for what? For failure? He must now make one of two decisions, either to give up his hope of being God's man, or to go forward knowing that there was nothing ahead of him but apparent failure. It is at this moment that the greatness of the man is revealed. He chose to go forward into "failure," and as we read his story there is nothing to show us any different picture.

Certainly he wrote great and marvelous prophecies, but they were not the action stories we might expect. Everything the Lord said came true. No one listened; there was no response; every year was the same—nothing to show for all the "blood, toil, tears, and sweat."

But that is the whole point of the message, "Success is obedience to the known, revealed will of God, regardless of the consequences." Isaiah was totally true and obedient, regardless of the consequences, and so, in the sight of the Lord, Isaiah was a great success. I call it "the success of failure." What courage it must have taken to continue day after day, with no hope of apparent impact or response. Anybody can serve when all is well and the results are there to see, but it takes a hero to slog it out, year after year, and still trust and rest in the Lord.

This is where this chapter would be a help to some of you who are reading these words. Many of us are "little nobodies," living our lives in our own little ways. Sometimes we may see success, as the world sees it, but very often we have little to show for our years of toil. Some of you are parents who have struggled so hard to raise a family in whom you could have a great pride, but what are you seeing now? Failure? Heartache?

Some of you are pastors or Christian workers, and you have poured your life into your ministry or your Sunday School, only to see so little reward for all your efforts.

Stand alongside of Isaiah and see as never before what success is in God's eyes. Your success is your obedience, your continuing struggle in spite of all your disappointments. When your eyes are off the consequences and your heart is obedient to your Lord, that is success, glorious success!

It came to me recently, as I was reading some of the marvelous passages in Isaiah where he speaks of comfort and encouragement, that he was writing about himself. The choice of words which are jewels of joy to those who are lonely and crushed were first of all applied in his own life.

Just imagine what the following messages would mean to this brave soul living in his lonely world of failure. "Thou wilt keep him in perfect peace, whose mind is stayed on thee: because he trusteth in thee" (26:3).

"Fear thou not; for I am with thee: be not dismayed, for I am thy God: I will strengthen thee; yea, I will help thee; yea, I will uphold thee with the right hand of my righteousness" (41:10).

"I will bring the blind by a way that they knew not; I will lead them in paths that they have not known: I will make darkness light before them, and crooked things straight. These things will I do unto them, and not forsake them" (42:16).

"And even to your old age I am he; and even to hoar hairs will I carry you: I have made, and I will bear; even I will carry, and will deliver you" (46:4).

As we study the Bible, we find that Isaiah was not the only servant who started his life's work with nothing but the promise of failure. Jeremiah, too, is a fascinating study along the same lines. In chapter 1 we see the Lord calling him to his life's work, but Jeremiah protested that he was too young. "Then said I, Ah, Lord God! behold, I cannot speak: for I am a child" (v. 6). The Lord overruled his excuses, and we read something similar to the experience of Isaiah. "Then the Lord put forth his hand and touched my mouth. And the Lord said unto me, Behold I have put my words in thy mouth" (v. 9).

The rest of chapter 1 describes prospects similar to those the Lord offered Isaiah, a future of struggling and preaching to a people who would not listen. It is a challenging thing to realize that, in obedience to the will of God, Jeremiah preached for over forty years to the people of Jerusalem and Judah without seeing any national result. He warned the people, telling how God would destroy Jerusalem. They laughed at him, telling him Jerusalem was God's Holy City and God would not destroy his own city.

Then Jeremiah threatened that unless the people turned back from their sins to serve the Lord, the same Lord would destroy his holy Temple. This, they replied, was crazy; God would not destroy his holy Temple!

So it went on year by year, for forty years! The story of Jeremiah is a countdown to destruction, for the day eventually came when we walked through the burning streets of Jerusalem, with Solomon's golden Temple going up in flames, and the streets littered with the corpses of those who refused to listen, much less to obey.

And that was Jeremiah's life story, ending in the total destruction of his own people. All his forty years seemed a waste of time, with nothing to show but national failure. And yet that was what the Lord promised him. Again it was the success of failure—because the obedience was Jeremiah's part; the consequences were God's part.

We can see the same sequence in the beginning of the story of Ezekiel. In chapters 2 and 3 he is sent to a people who will not listen or obey. Listen to the Lord speaking in 3:7. "But the house of Israel will not hearken unto thee: for they will not hearken unto me; for all the house of Israel are impudent and hardhearted."

Then, to use our modern expressions, the Lord told Ezekiel he would be banging his head against a stone wall. What a prospect for a young man just commencing his life's ministry! No wonder we read in 3:14, "So the spirit lifted me up, and took me away, and I went in bitterness, in the heat of my spirit; but the hand of the Lord was strong upon me."

I find it challenging to realize that the three major prophets were young men whose life ministries were destined to failure from the beginning. How true are the words in Isaiah 55:8. "For my thoughts are not your thoughts, neither are your ways my ways, saith the Lord."

But their apparent failure was the proof of their success, because that is how the Lord planned it all!

Now take another look at your own life. This time don't measure it by the world's standards, but by the standards and values of an eternal God who knows the end from the beginning. Every measure of your obedience is the measure of your success. And if that obedience is maintained in the face of apparent failure, you have joined the ranks of the noble saints of old.

So, take heart, my brother, my sister, as you face this first question from the Lord himself, "What seek ye?" "What are you looking for in life?" Your answer can be, I am looking for success, God's way. I want to be obedient to the known revealed will of God for me, regardless of the consequences." The obedience is your business. The consequences are God's business!

A Prayer of Meditation

Dear Father, thank you for showing me what real success is. Forgive me that I so often think it must be "bigger and better."

Thank you, Father, for every occasion when I can see results that encourage me. How grateful I am!

Teach me, dear Lord, to concentrate on the obedience part and to leave the consequences to you.

Thank you, Lord, for calling me into your family. Touch my lips. Speak through my mouth. Train me, Lord, to be able to stand in the light of your holiness, and may the result be to your greater glory.

10.
"Wilt Thou Be Made Whole?"

Let us look at another question Jesus asked. Once more it seems so simple, almost unimportant. When we dig into the question and the story, though, we will discover some wonderful truths that could change your life.

John 5:1-9 tells the story of the Lord's visit to the pool of Bethesda. (The name *Bethesda* means house of mercy.) Immediately we meet a remarkable situation. The place was crowded with people in dire need of physical help, but we know of only one who was healed. Why was there mercy for only one when so much need was there? Why didn't the Lord heal them all? He could have done so, but he did not. He went to one man only. This is an illustration of the sovereignty of God in action.

So often we want to ask why God does not heal the needs that we can see. Some conditions are so painful that it seems almost cruel to leave the conditions unaltered. It will always be true that, "My thoughts are not your thoughts, neither are your ways my ways, saith the Lord" (Isa. 55:8). The sovereignty of God is the secret of God. Sometimes he unfolds his secrets; often he does not. And we are left to trust and to obey.

In describing the needy people gathered at the pool, John speaks of four different classes—impotent or the weak, blind, halt, withered. As I meditate on these groups I see them as those with no power, no vision, no walk, and no fruit. They were all God's people, but each one had a deep need.

Somehow this reminds me of what I find in many of the churches where I minister to God's people, born-again believers gathered together in church, the house of mercy. Some have no power in their lives; others have no vision for the things of God. Many have no sure walk. They stumble on through life, spending their Christian experience picking themselves up from the floor of failure. The fourth group live barren, fruitless lives—years of living and nothing to show for it.

The man in the story had been thirty-eight years in a powerless, walkless, fruitless condition, and all the time the place was called the house of mercy. The thought is almost ironic—misery in the house of mercy. Yet that is how many of God's people are today.

As we move on into the story, let the Holy Spirit seek you and search you. Are you without real power in your Christian life? Has your vision dimmed, or did you ever see through the eyes of God? How about your daily walk? Are you bearing fruit as you should or are you just withered? Don't be afraid to be honest in these areas. The Lord knows your condition and your need. If you can own up and agree with his diagnosis, then there is hope of real blessing for you.

The chapter begins by speaking of "a feast of the Jews" (v. 1) in Jerusalem. The time was one of rejoicing and of praising the Lord, but there was no joy at the Pool of Bethesda—just a crowd of needy, suffering people waiting for the moving of the water, waiting to be healed of whatever disease they had.

The Lord came to this mass of seeking people. He was seeking also. He came to one man who for thirty-eight years had been powerless to walk. What a story must have been his! How did he get to the pool? Who fed him? Where did he go at night?

Then we read these wonderful words, "When Jesus saw him lie, and knew that he had been now a long time in that case, he saith to him, Wilt thou be made whole?" The Lord knew his situation and his suffering. He came with all the majesty of divine power and asked the amazing question, "Would you like to be made whole, completely and totally healed?" (AT).

At first we think, *What an unnecessary question to ask! Why, of course he wanted to be healed. Why else would he be lying there day after day?*

Notice what the Lord asked and was offering—total healing! He was not offering to patch up the man, or to make him crutches, or to teach him to crawl, but a complete wholeness.

Realize that this is what the Lord does when he brings salvation to a needy soul who receives him as personal Savior. God is not concerned with patching-up human failure, or providing spiritual crutches on which to hobble. God's salvation reaches to the whole person—spirit, soul and body.

Second Corinthians 5:17-18 tells us, "Therefore if any man be in Christ, he is a new creature: old things are passed away; behold all things are become new. And all things are of God."

I remember once at our conference center during a special week for teenagers, a young girl came to me with a message from her mother. He mother wanted her daughter to have enough religion to make her respectable, but not too much to make her uncomfortable. Those were her very sentiments—to be respectable, but not uncomfortable.

God's salvation is not designed to make people simply respectable. In fact, God is not concerned in simply making people good, or turning out better people. God's plan is to make new people! He makes them new by making them whole.

This is one of the great differences between humanism and the gospel. Humanism works from the outside and is aimed at making better people. In theory it sounds marvelous—providing better surroundings, better living conditions, better education, all with the object of improving people. Thank God for every means whereby people are helped to live a better life, but that is not enough. The change does not come from the outside.

The gospel speaks of a Savior who comes into the human heart by his Holy Spirit and works from within producing a new kind of humanity, whereby the individual is made a partaker of the divine nature (2 Pet. 1:4).

The great proof of this is to see this same gospel in action in the days of the early church moving into the lives of people who were socially, educationally, and economically destitute—slaves in a totalitarian state. There was no change in their social, education, or economic position, but they were changed in the inside—born again—new creatures in Christ. As such they "turned the world upside down" (Acts 17:6). The impact of their changed lives was devastating on the world structure in those days.

History has repeated the same message again and again. God's aim is to make people whole on the inside. Then through them he can change the world. This is what he is seeking to do through your life: first to make you whole and change you; then through you to change the world where you are. This is why this question is so vital to your life at this time. There are many believers who have experienced part of God's salvation but who, as yet, have never been made whole.

We thought before that, in one sense, the question the Lord asked was unnecessary. Of course the man wanted to be healed. Why else was he there day after day?

If the question sounds strange, just see how much more strange was the reply given by the man. We would imagine his answer would be a decided yes; of course he wanted to be made whole! But see what he actually said, "Sir, I have no man, when the water is troubled, to put me into the pool: but while I am coming, another steppeth down before me" (v. 7). He actually began making excuses for his present condition, almost as if he were justifying his physical weakness. Instead of answering with a simple yes, he poured out an apologetic, "Because."

We have no idea how long he had been lying at the pool of Bethesda, but one thing we do know. He was always where the action was, but he never got involved with the blessing!

This is how many believers are in our churches, especially in those fine churches where God is doing a great work. They, too, are always where the action is, but they never get involved.

Could this be a picture of your life? The man in the story was content to be a failure. He accepted failure as normal and was totally surprised when the Lord offered him a new capacity for living, to be made whole.

Notice the actual words of our Lord, "Wilt thou be made whole?" (v. 6). You cannot make yourself whole. Somebody has to make you whole. I meet Christians who are working hard trying to make themselves whole. They read books, attend meetings, get involved with special seminars and workshops, all in good faith, all with the ultimate object of tracing what is missing in their lives so that they can put it right and make themselves whole. Their desires and intentions are praiseworthy, but their methods and techniques are at fault. Once again we remind ourselves, "My thoughts are not your thoughts, neither are your ways my ways, saith the Lord" (Isa. 55:8).

Obviously the message contained in the story is that only Christ can make a person whole. That is as true today as it was in New Testament times. Notice the miraculous nature of the healing of this man who had not walked for thirty-eight years: "Immediately the man was made whole, and took up his bed, and walked" (v. 9). If you have ever spent some time in bed, unable to get out, you will remember the first time you tried to stand and walk. Your legs were like jelly, and you almost had to learn to balance and walk again. Just consider how this man could stand, after thirty-eight years, then roll up his mat, then stride out and walk! What a glorious miracle!

As we dig a little deeper into the story, I want to show you that being made whole involves a twofold relationship with the Lord Jesus. This is necessary because in the economy of God's salvation he has offered the Lord Jesus in a twofold way. If we are only involved with half of what is offered, then we can only enjoy half a salvation. This condition of taking only half of what God gives results in believers being saved yet experiencing no capacity to live strong, robust lives. They are believers with no power, no vision, no walk, and no fruit! These people are where the action is, but they are never involved. They have accepted defeat as normal.

This being so, you can see now how vital this message is in your Christian experience. "Would you like to be made whole?" Colossians 2:9-10 says "In [Christ] dwelleth all the fulness of the Godhead, bodily. And ye are complete in him." Notice the emphasis here: "Ye are complete in him," here and now. This is not something you experience in heaven; this is a 'here and now' experience. You are complete for service, for suffering, for joy, for fear, for frustration. Whatever experience or situation comes your way, you are complete. You need no more experiences, no more excitement, no more deeper teaching—you are complete in Christ. But you will only avail yourself of that completeness when you avail yourself of all that God gives through Christ.

Let me explain further. When we were sinners, without God, without Christ, and without hope in the world, our prime need was a Savior who could save us from our sin and guilt. So we read in John 3:16: "For God so loved the world, that he gave his only begotten Son, that whosoever believeth in him should not perish, but have everlasting life."

Thus we read of the Lord Jesus being given for us, "Who his own self bear our sins in his own body on the tree" (1 Pet. 2:24). This is the first way the Lord Jesus was given, and, as we acknowledge our sin, repent of our sin, and open our hearts to receive him as our own personal Savior, then we are forgiven, born again, and become new creatures in Christ. The death of Christ qualifies me to go to heaven as a forgiven sinner. In that sense, the gift of Christ by his saving death makes me fit for heaven. I am accepted in the Beloved.

Now this is true for every sinner who has been saved by the death of Christ. But that is only half of what God has for us in his glorious plan of salvation. Not only did the Lord Jesus die for me on the cross, but he rose again and comes to indwell me by his Holy Spirit. Always remember that the Holy Spirit's work is to make Christ real in the heart and life of the believer.

You will remember Paul says, "I can do all things through Christ which strengthenth me" (Phil. 4:13). "For me to live is Christ, and to die is gain (Phil. 1:21). He never said "for me to live is the Holy Spirit," or "I can do all things through the Holy Spirit." The Christian life for Paul was a day by day relationship with the risen, victorious Christ who indwelt him through the presence of the Holy Spirit. That is why he says in Galatians 2:20, "I am crucified with Christ: nevertheless I live; yet not I, but Christ liveth in me: and the life which I now live in the flesh I live by the faith of the Son of God, who loved me, and gave himself for me."

It is this glorious day-by-day experience of the risen, victorious Christ, indwelling by his Holy Spirit, which is missing in so many Christian lives. They accept his saving death, and they are thus fit for heaven; but they have no vital relationship, no intimate sense of the indwelling Christ. He is in their lives; they are complete in Christ; but they have never realized the sheer wonder of his presence. The saving death of Christ makes me fit for heaven, but the saving life of Christ indwelling me makes me fit for earth!

There are many believers who are fit for heaven, but they are not fit for earth. They cannot handle life. They have no power, no vision, no walk, and no fruit. They need to be made whole, complete, to move into the full plan of God for their lives. They need no additional blessing, no additional baptism, just a realization that they are complete in Christ. They need to possess their possessions, make Christ real, to practice the presence of Christ day by day.

You say, "How does it work? What do I do?" Let me tell you how I seek to live each day. Each morning when I awake I draw near to the Lord in prayer. I thank him for the gift of the new day. Then I say words like these. "Thank you, Lord Jesus, that you dwell in my heart. You said you would never leave me nor forsake me. Dear Lord, I can face anything that comes into my life today because you are there to handle it for me and through me."

As I face my problems and fears I can say, "Lord Jesus, I cannot handle these situations. I can't, but you can! That is why you indwell me. Dear Lord, I want to commit this day to you. As I go on, may I know your presence and your peace!" You can pray likewise.

Then throughout the day practice his presence. Speak to him; commit your ways unto him, and he will direct your path.

Don't fall into the trap of *trying* to live for Jesus. It sounds good and noble, but it is not scriptural. It is not part of God's plan. The devil has many Christians slogging away, day by day, *trying* to live for Jesus. You will never make it, and God doesn't ask it.

Let me ask you one simple question. "Did you die for Jesus?" The answer is obvious. Of course you didn't; he died for you! Well, if you did not die for him, why are you trying to live for him?" The one who died for you now wants *to live in you, and for you, and through you,* day by day.

When I realize the twofold work of Christ, that this work makes me complete in Christ, then I can go on to enjoy being made whole in Christ. I not only have my sins forgiven and a home in heaven; I also have the sense of his life living in me now. I am fit for heaven and fit for earth!

The saving death of Christ is the finished work of Christ, "One sacrifice for sins for ever" (Heb. 10:12). The saving life of Christ, as he indwells me, never to leave me, is the unfolding work of Christ: "He which hath begun a good work in you will perform it [make an end of it, complete it] until the day of Jesus Christ" (Phil. 1:6).

Let him finish what he began!

If you are interested in becoming vitally involved with the living Christ, let me draw your attention to the lesson God taught in Jeremiah 18:1-6. "The word which came to Jeremiah from the Lord, saying, Arise, and go down to the potter's house, . . . and behold he wrought a work on the wheels. And the vessel that he made of clay was marred in the hand of the potter: so he made it again another

"WILT THOU BE MADE WHOLE?"

vessel, as seemed good to the potter to make it. Then the word of the Lord came to me saying, . . . cannot I do with you, as this potter? saith the Lord, Behold as the clay is in the potter's hand, so are ye in my hand."

Let this picture speak to you in all its simplicity. The vessel was marred. Something went wrong, but even so, it was still in the hand of the potter. Is there something wrong, something missing in your life? Remember you are still in God's hands!

Now notice what happened. The clay was yielded to the hand of the potter, and he made it again, "as seemed good to the potter to make it."

God can remold your life as seems good to him, if you will yield your life to his hands.

When I was in India I learned three things from an old Indian potter. First the clay had to be soft. Second, the hands of the potter had to stay on the clay. Third, the wheel had to be turning under the control of the potter.

If you want to experience the wholeness that only Christ can bring then you must see yourself in this powerful illustration. Your life must be soft as the clay was soft—no hard areas of disobedience and stubbornness. Then you must yield yourself and see yourself as always in his hands. Never seek to escape from the hands of the Potter. The result will be a total collapse of any structure he is fashioning.

Lastly, let him turn the wheel of your life. If he is in complete control, then his hands work in conjunction with the speed of the turning wheel. They will never be out of step. The result will be as perfect as you allow the Potter to make it. Don't tell him what to do. Let the Potter refashion your life as seems good to him to make it.

Here then is the question of the Lord to you, "Would you like to be made whole? Would you like me to make you whole?"

A Prayer of Meditation

Heavenly Father, I bow in worship and adoration.

By faith I come now to you, Lord Jesus, the Divine Potter. I want you to make me whole. I want to know and experience the wonder of your risen life in me, controlling, guiding, fashioning anew.

Lord, I would be as soft, malleable clay in your hands. If necessary, may my tears of repentance soften the hardness of my heart.

Let me never leave you. Oh, may I know the nearness of your hands—the pierced hands. In those hands there is safety and security and a sense of life with a purpose.

Lord Jesus, I yield to you not only the clay but the wheel of my life. May it turn as seems best to you. Whether fast or slow, may it be in conjunction with those blessed hands, and may the result be another vessel, as seems good to the Potter to make it.

11.
"Where Are the Nine?"

When we talk about "The Good Samaritan" we usually think of the story told by the Lord as recorded in Luke 10:30-37. The Good Samaritan was the only one who had compassion on the victim who "fell among thieves." There are other Samaritans who are equally worthy of that title. There is the woman who lived in Sychar, who met Jesus at the well. She comes into the story as "The Bad Samaritan," who was "The Sad Samaritan," who became "The Glad Samaritan," who brought revival to her own town.

We meet a special character in Luke 17:11-19. The Lord was passing through Samaria, and as he journeyed, "There met him ten men that were lepers, which stood afar off" (v. 12). These ten men were obeying the instructions given in the Word of God, they "stood afar off." Because they were lepers, they had lost many of the privileges of human life. They were unclean and, as such, were cast out of normal society. They were strangers to their loved ones, living in the lepers' world of loathsome degradation.

Into their hopeless world came the Son of God. "And they lifted up their voices, and said, Jesus, Master, have mercy on us" (v. 12). Normally, they would have been begging for money or for food, enough to sustain them in their misery. This time their cry was for mercy. They must have had a high appreciation of the person and work of the Lord, because, recognizing their wretched condition, they immediately cried to him for mercy.

The response was instant and without question, just the simple directive, "Go shew yourselves unto the priests" (v. 14). In the councils of God the priests were the ones who not only dealt with the disease of sin in the soul, they were also the medical authorities who dealt with all forms of physical uncleanness—chief of which was leprosy.

Then comes a beautiful verse, "And it came to pass, that as they went, they were cleansed" (v. 14). The simple directive of Christ was followed by a simple act of faith on the part of these ten men. It was when they acted in faith and set off in their leprosy that the cleansing came. If they had stood there waiting for something to happen, the story could have had a different ending. As it was, they fulfilled the necessary qualification for blessing—they trusted and obeyed—and the healing was theirs.

Then comes the lovely part of the story: "One of them, when he saw that he was healed, turned back, and with a loud voice glorified God. And fell down on his face at his feet, giving him thanks: and he was a Samaritan" (vv. 15-16).

What infinite joy must have flooded the hearts of these ten men as they ran and felt the surge of wholesome cleanliness surging through their bodies! How eager they would have been to appear before the priest and receive from him consent to return to normal life, to go home, to embrace, to live again. The mercy of God had opened the doors to a new life. But one of them was so overwhelmed by the goodness of God, that in spite of his desire to return to life, he returned to the Lord and "fell down on his face at his feet, giving him thanks" (v. 16).

At this point the Lord asked his searching question. "Were there not ten cleansed? but where are the nine? There are not found that returned to give glory to God, save this stranger" (vv. 17-18). What disappointment is revealed in those words, "Where are the nine?" They were ready to trust and obey, ready to return to life, but their response was entirely selfish. It was true they were healed and restored. They had received their share of the blessing, but the Lord Jesus was left where they had found him, ignored and unthanked. It was almost as if the nine lepers had taken him for granted, that it was his job to show mercy.

As they hurried on their way to the priest, they were identifying themselves with religion in its outward forms and ceremonies. All they did was correct and in accordance with the law, but something was missing. The Samaritan who returned to the Lord was showing an in-depth relationship with reality. The nine were demonstrating an outward relationship with religion.

This is where the question asked by the Lord can challenge us today. "Where are the nine?" Are we like the nine who came to Christ for healing and forgiveness? Do we then go our way and become involved simply with organized religion? Or are we like the stranger? Having been blessed and healed, do we come to the Lord with our worship and adoration to "fall down on [our] face[s] . . . giving him thanks"?

I am deeply concerned these days with the whole question of our thankfulness to the Lord, not only the question, but the quality. Our society is becoming more soulless and impersonal as the days go by. When men and women become numbers hidden away in a computer, something lovely and fragrant disappears from our life-style. You do not thank machines, however intricate and expensive they may be. You just respond to the pressing of the button, like a piece of human machinery.

The whole subject of thankfulness is emphasized repeatedly in the Word of God, in every area. Romans 1 speaks of this in relation to "all ungodliness and unrighteousness of men" (v. 18). It states that "When they knew God, they glorified him not as God, neither were thankful" (v. 21). Incidentally, if you compare these words with the response of the Samaritan, you will notice that he glorified God and was thankful.

I want to develop this idea of the importance of thankfulness and to show how you may be missing out on much of God's additional blessing by an absence of real, dedicated, constant thankfulness in your life.

Second Corinthians 9:8 is one of the superlative promises contained in God's Word, "God is able to make all grace abound toward you; that ye, always having all sufficiency in all things, may abound to every good work." See how confidently the promise begins, "God is able." Man has no part in this. If he had, there would be doubts, conditions, and exceptions. But it is not so with God. God is able. Then follows what I call the five "alls" of certainty. No area is left uncovered: "all grace"; "always"; "all sufficiency"; "all things"; "all good work." The inclusiveness of these words is magnificent, especially when they follow the words, "God is able."

Having realized that this is the unqualified promise of God, undeserved and unearned by us, the problem then arises as to why the lives of so many Christians are devoid of this grace and this sufficiency. Like the nine lepers in the story, they recognize their need as sinners. They cry to the Lord for mercy; they are forgiven, restored, healed, and born again. They then become involved with religion in a church-related relationship. But from then on, many of them experience powerless lives devoid of any sparkle of spiritual reality.

The answer to the absence can be found in verse 15 of 2 Corinthians 9. "Thanks be unto God for his unspeakable gift." The word translated here as "unspeakable" is a word rich in volume and color. This is one of those places where Paul finds it impossible to tell in human language the glory and magnificent wonder of the reality he is seeking to communicate. Here he is telling about the gift that God has given—the Lord Jesus Christ, Son of God, Savior of the world.

In one sense the quality of life that I live day by day depends upon one thing only—my appreciation of the Lord Jesus Christ in all the manifold outreaches of God's plan of salvation and my attitude of constant thankfulness for such a precious possession.

Let me tell you a story to show you what I mean. Some time ago I was in Brazil speaking at a small Bible school for nationals, most of whom spoke only Portuguese. One girl spoke a little English, so I was able to counsel with her concerning the failure in her Christian life. She was full of good intentions, but was equally dominated by areas of weakness, fear, and temper. I had the privilege of telling her more about the person and work of the Lord Jesus, about his saving death on the cross (which she knew), and about his saving life as he indwells us through his Holy Spirit.

When I was leaving, she slipped a little note into my pocket. Let me give you an exact copy of what she wrote.

> Mr. Hunter:
> God spoke through you for me. My name is Sonia Maria, a Brazilian girl with 19 years old!
> I was frustrated with my Christian life, wanting to leave the Bible Institute.
> Now I know how Jesus can be real to myself.
> Seems to me that God drove you here only to speak with me!
> I want to express you my new joy and peace.
> I hope Jesus will guide me in that new step of faith!
> I was afraid to go on, but now I don't have any more!
> My Jesus was little, but now He is growing up.

"WHERE ARE THE NINE?"

> It's the first time that I'm studying the Bible here.
> I'll speak with you about how the Christ is winning in my life only in the heavens,
> so . . . Good-bye!
> > with love in Christ,
> > Sonia Maria
> > Isaiah 41:10.

If you want an added blessing, study the verse she gave me, Isaiah 41:10. It meant much to her.

This note has blessed my life. I have never seen her, or heard from her since that day. As she said, she can tell me in heaven how Jesus won in her life.

I have always remembered the lovely way she expressed her new appreciation and relationship with the Lord Jesus, "My Jesus was little, but now He is growing up."

As I wrote before, the quality of life you live day by day depends upon one thing—how big is your Jesus? Is he little in your life? Is he growing up?

We considered in the previous chapter the twofold work of Christ: on the cross, his saving death; in the crises, his saving life. These two aspects of the life and ministry of the Lord are part of that unspeakable gift we read about in 2 Corinthains 9:15.

There is only one thing which releases for me the wonder and power of the death of Christ. That is my attitude of thankfulness in word and in deed. In like manner there is one thing only which releases for me the added wonder and power of the saving life of Christ as he indwells me by his Holy Spirit. That is, again, my attitude of thankfulness, constant thankfulness, day by day, in word and in deed.

Let me show you how this can work out in practice in your life, each day. Look with me in 1 Thessalonians 5:6-19, "Rejoice evermore. Pray without ceasing. In every thing give thanks: for this is the will of God in Christ Jesus concerning you. Quench not the Spirit."

Remember, we are considering the question of the Lord, "Where are the nine?" The absence of constant thankfulness can stultify a Christian life.

Notice in these verses what the will of God is for you, in Christ Jesus. "In every thing give thanks"—not in "some things," or in "most things," but "in every thing."

The preposition is of vital importance in this verse. It is not, "For every thing" but "In every thing." There is a quality of teaching which emphasizes the word *for*, which instructs me that whatever happens I must thank God for it. Whatever heartache, tragedy, or bereavement comes upon me, I must thank God for it! That is only partly true, as we shall see later on.

The teaching here is that in every situation, every tragedy, every joy, whatever may come my way, I am to thank God in the situation, not for the situation. For what do I thank him if sorrow strikes, if my world falls to pieces? I thank him for his unspeakable gift, for the Lord Jesus.

In the case of sorrow and tragedy, I thank him that the Lord said he would never leave me, never forsake me. I claim his indwelling Holy Spirit. I recognize his presence. I realize I am not alone, and I commit to him the situation with all its hopelessness. I tell him that I cannot face it alone, I cannot cope with it. I can't, but he can! By faith I commit it to him and leave it with him and go on into the heartache, believing that he is in control. That is the will of God in Christ Jesus concerning you. Remember, don't quench the Spirit. Allow him to overflow into all the areas of need.

In this way whatever happens, I can live in a constant state of thankfulness, always conscious of his presence, his power, and his peace.

I referred before to the teaching which emphasizes being thankful for everything. We have just seen that in the time of testing and teaching it is not "for," but "in" everything I give thanks. As time passes and the divine healing of the Holy Spirit mends my brokenness, there may come a time in my life, there should come a time, when looking back I can thank God for the sorrow. When events have subsided and the pieces have fallen into place, maybe I can see how all things did work together for good. By the wonderful gift of hindsight, everyone has 20-20 vision. There should be a day when I can say words which I have heard over and over again from hurt souls who have been healed. "When it happened my whole world fell to pieces and I was shattered, but now, looking back, I can thank the Lord for all that happened because he became real to me, and I came to know the Lord in a new and wonderful way."

Let me show you now the importance of thankfulness not only in practice, but in prayer. As you read these words, can you spot what is wrong? "Be careful for nothing, but in every thing by prayer and supplication let your requests be made known unto God. And the peace of God, which passeth all understanding, shall keep your hearts and minds through Christ Jesus."

It sounds correct, if you remember the King James Version, but it is not so, because two vital words are missing. The words are from Philippians 4:6-7. The original says, "but in every thing by prayer and supplication *with thanksgiving* let your requests be made known unto God." The prayers have to be made "with thanksgiving." Then "The peace of God, which passeth all understanding, shall keep [or garrison] your hearts and minds through Christ Jesus."

I meet many people whose prayers bring them no peace, either in heart or in mind. They are sincere and sometimes desperate and insistent, and yet they feel no sense of response on the part of God. Some become cynical and comment on the words, "the peace of God, which passeth all understanding." They say, "That is exactly what happens; it passes all understanding!"

And yet these instructions on prayer are the secret for peace and blessing, if we will only do what the Word says. There is a popular, humorous saying which goes, "When all else fails, read the instructions." This is what is necessary in this situation.

We are told to, "Be careful for nothing." Phillips puts it, "Don't worry over anything whatever." Then we are instructed how to handle the situations in order to find peace and experience the keeping power of the Lord. We are told to bring our prayer with thanksgiving. What does that mean?

In one sense there are two kinds of prayers, the "asking prayers" and the "thanking prayers." This section is emphasizing the importance of praying "with thanksgiving."

Asking prayers are often very negative. They prove we do not have it, and there is a doubt that we might get it.

Thanking prayers should always be very positive. Let me show you what I mean. I sometimes hear people praying desperately to God for special strength and power to meet a certain situation—just a little extra power would be such a help. But God has no need to answer such prayers. The provision has already been made.

The Lord Jesus said, "All power is given unto me in heaven and in earth. . . . and, lo I am with you alway even unto the end of the world" (Matt. 28:18,20). The Lord has all the power and the authority, and he indwells me, never to leave me. My prayer, with thanksgiving, should be made, first telling the Lord the need in my life, then acknowledging my inability to meet that need.

Now comes the thanksgiving. I thank the Lord that he has all the power ("Greater is he that is in you, than he that is in the world," 1 John 4:4), and that he indwells me, that God is able to make all grace abound toward me so that I will always have all sufficiency in all things at all times.

Finally, I commit to his indwelling Holy Spirit that area which has caused all the concern. By faith I thank him for what he will yet do, and so I allow the peace of God to keep my heart and my mind, by the same Christ Jesus.

This practice of prayer needs constant attention and a constant deep sense of thankfulness to the Lord Jesus for all he is to me as my own personal Savior. "Thanks be unto God, for his unspeakable gift."

In this way, there will always be a positive answer to that sad, searching question of the Lord, "Where are the nine?" We will be constantly thanking him first for all that he is, and then for all that he has done, and is doing, and will do.

This is the secret of dynamic living and dynamic praying.

A Prayer for Meditation

Heavenly Father, I sometimes feel that I am one of the nine who took all there was, then went their own ways. Forgive me, Lord, for my ingratitude.

How marvelous is your provision to me, and for me. Thank you for dying for me and thank you also for living for me as you indwell me with your Holy Spirit.

Teach me, Lord, in everything to give thanks for all that you are at that moment, in that situation.

Teach me to pray with thanksgiving. Let me draw on all the resources I have in you.

Deliver me from trying to handle things in my own small strength. May I be strong in the strength of another — of you!

Thank you, Lord Jesus.

12.
"Believest Thou This?"

The story in this chapter is centered on the special family that lived in Bethany. The family was special for several reasons. First, their home was the place where the Lord Jesus loved to stay, where he was always loved and welcomed. The account is found in John 11:1-46.

It was special also because of the three who lived there—two sisters and one brother. There is no mention of husbands for the sisters or a wife for the brother. This of itself was most unusual. Marriage was considered the natural and normal way of life in those days, and children were the blessing from the Lord. Some traditions have it that Martha may have been the wife or widow of Simon the Leper.

But there were no children in this house, no husbands, no wife. In one sense those who lived there were exceedingly dependent on one another for human love and support.

This is one reason why the Lord was so welcome in their midst. He brought the sense of completeness and security. Somehow he would fill the empty space in their unusual lives, and their tender love for him would bring a sweet fragrance of human devotion to his busy life.

His response to their devotion is shown in John 11:5, "Now Jesus loved Martha, and her sister, and Lazarus."

It is interesting to note that the Bible names only two other people of whom it is specifically recorded that Jesus loved them. One was the rich young ruler in Mark 10:21, and the other was the apostle John who called himself "the disciple whom Jesus loved" in John 13:23; 19:26; 21:7,20.

What comfort and joy and peace must have surrounded the Lord as he stayed in that blessed home! The fact of this mutual love only serves to emphasize the unusual response of the Lord to the message he received from the two sisters, "Lord, behold, he whom thou lovest is sick" (John 11:3).

In spite of his love for these three precious people, he chose to let them go through the intimate agony of seeing a loved one die, and endure the hopeless misery of committing a much loved body to the grave.

He said, "This sickness is not unto death, but for the glory of God, that the Son of God might be glorified thereby"(v. 4).

To all those who truly love the Lord Jesus these words can come with a startling challenge. The ultimate purpose of all suffering, if I am prepared to trace it through to the end, is eventually for the glory of God, that the Son of God might be glorified thereby. This great truth can give us a new approach to human suffering, and can open new doors for comfort and understanding.

As we proceed with this story we will come to the question that the Lord asked Martha. For the present we need to see the quality of love and human relationship existing between the Lord and these three and the depth of understanding in the hearts of the two sisters.

The fact that the Lord allowed these sisters to suffer is underlined in verses 14 and 15, "Then said Jesus unto them plainly, Lazarus is dead. And I am glad for your sakes that I was not there, to the intent ye may believe."

In the amazing councils of God, the Lord Jesus allowed this suffering to run its full, agonizing course so that disciples might believe. In the awesome providences of God our own sufferings are never wasted. There may be someone, somewhere who could be learning to believe as they see our response to tragedy and heartache.

There were many dramatic moments as this story unfolded. One of the most moving must have been when Martha heard of the coming of Jesus and when she met him before he even reached their home.

How sorrowful and hopeless were her first words, "Lord, if thou hadst been here, my brother had not died." Then there came words revealing her knowledge and faith in Jesus, "But I know that even now whatsoever thou wilt ask of God, God will give it thee" (vv. 21-22).

Behind the brokenness was a belief reaching out to touch the unknown and unseen.

"BELIEVEST THOU THIS?"

The Lord gently led her on, "Thy brother shall rise again" (v. 23). To this truth Martha agreed, but that was something for the "last day" (v. 24).

Then from the lips of Christ came words which have, down the ages, brought courage and everlasting comfort to millions, "I am the resurrection, and the life: he that believeth in me, though he were dead, yet shall he live: And whosoever liveth and believeth in me shall never die" (vv. 25-26a).

Martha was the first person ever to hear those words of divine authority so inclusive in their truth.

Then followed the words which form the title of this chapter. Having pronounced these awe-inspiring words Jesus asked, "Believest thou this?" (v. 26b).

As we look into this question, and the ramifications leading from it, I am praying that the Lord, by his Holy Spirit, will guide our hearts into new areas of truth whereby a new sense of joy and assurance can be brought into our lives.

Martha's immediate answer to the Lord's question was the great confession of her faith, "Yea, Lord: I believe that thou art the Christ, the Son of God, which should come unto the world" (v. 27). What a tremendous moment, almost a terrifying moment, as she stood in his presence and proclaimed his deity—that he was truly the Messiah, and that he was actually the Son of God!

And yet, as great, wonderful, and marvelous as her words were, they did not answer the question asked by the Lord.

The whole point of this chapter is to see how we, too, can have a great faith and make a glorious confession and still fail to answer the searching question, "Believest thou this?"

The Lord was seeking an answer to the truths he proclaimed in verses 25 and 26. He was speaking about a twofold act of belief. The first was the belief of one who was dead. The second was the belief of one who was alive.

In verse 25 the Lord said, "He that believeth in me, though he were dead, yet shall he live." The reference here, regarding God's plan of salvation, is to the one who is dead, spiritually dead, in trespasses and sins. When such a one believes in Christ, he becomes alive, he is born again. As we read in Ephesians 2:1, "You hath he quickened [or made alive], who were dead in trespasses and sins."

This is describing the experience which many people call "being saved," which Jesus called "being born again." The first time we are born we are physically and mentally alive, but spiritually dead. When we are "born again," the second time, we receive spiritual life.

All true believers have had this experience. They are saved, born again. They were dead; they believed in Christ; they became alive. This is what the Lord was speaking of in verse 25.

But verse 26 is speaking of something entirely different, "Whosoever liveth and believeth in me shall never die." Here is someone who has become alive. By faith this person has accepted Christ as personal Savior. He has passed from death to life, and now, as one who is alive, he keeps on believing in Christ. Jesus said that such a one "shall never die." Instead, he experiences a conscious, everlasting relationship with the living Christ. As Paul said in 2 Corinthians 5:6, when we walk by faith even death is just being absent from the body to be present with the Lord. Such continuing belief opens the door to a new world of living. It is simple faith in Christ, in all his fullness of salvation.

Once again the great truths told in the previous chapters of the twofold work of Christ are repeated. God gave the Lord Jesus to die for me on the cross. When I believe this and receive him into my life as my own personal Savior, then I pass from death unto life; I am born again. I become a child of God. "The Spirit itself beareth witness with our spirit, that we are children of God" (Rom. 8:16). My human spirit which was spiritually dead becomes alive as his Spirit comes to indwell my spirit. Always remember Romans 8:9. "Now if any man have not the Spirit of Christ, he is none of his."

This is what happens when one believes for the first time and receives all the blessings of his saving death. But verse 26 tells what happens when one comes as a believer and keeps on believing in Christ. Believing means receiving—as we read in John 1:12, "But as many as received him, to them gave he power to become the sons of God, even to them that believe on his name."

When we keep on believing in Christ, we keep on receiving from Christ. The Word of God constantly urges us to go on with Christ. The verse that changed my life was Colossians 2:6, "As ye have therefore received Christ Jesus the Lord, so walk ye in him." How did I begin my Christian life? By receiving Christ as my own personal Savior. How do I continue? The same way I began, by continuing to receive Christ into my life day by day. What happens when I do this?

"BELIEVEST THOU THIS?"

I experience a glorious, continued relationship, as Paul said, "For me to live is Christ, and to die is gain" (Phil:1:21). In that sense, "Whosoever liveth and believeth on me shall never die" (John 11:26a). Believers keep on living with Christ. The position is the same. Only the place is different!

How does the believer keep on believing? In what does he believe? He receives all the potential of the saving life of Christ. As we have already seen, he learns to say "Thank you," both in practice and in prayer.

The test for us at this very moment is, "Believest thou this?" (v. 26b).

The tragedy is that many believers say like Martha, "Yea, Lord: I believe that thou art the Christ, the Son of God, which should come into the world" (v. 27). It is a glorious confession, but it does not answer the question.

The real content of Martha's belief was shown when it was put to the test (vv. 39-40).

The Lord ordered the stone to be taken away from the tomb, but Martha objected strongly. Four days of corruption will turn the loveliest body into something totally repulsive.

The Lord answered, "Said I not unto thee, that, if thou wouldest believe, thou shouldest see the glory of God?" (v. 40).

Continuing to believe always brings the possibility of seeing the glory of God. Paul indicates something similar when he writes of God's plan for the believer in Colossians 1:27. Referring to God's plan as "the mystery" he says, "To whom God would make known what is the riches of the glory of this mystery . . . which is Christ in you, the hope of glory."

The saving death of Christ is "Christ for you." The saving life of Christ is "Christ in you."

The one who is spiritually dead needs to believe on the saving death of Christ for him on the cross.

The believer goes on still to believe, but his belief is in the saving life of Christ—Christ in him. And as he continues to rest and trust in the living Christ, he moves into the area of "the hope of glory" even here and now.

May I ask you, "Believest thou this?" (v. 27). "Said I not unto thee, that, if thou wouldest believe, thou shouldest see the glory of God?" (v. 40).

In connection with this whole idea of the believer going on with Christ, we can see an interesting analogy in the words used by the Lord before the tomb of Lazarus.

The Lord spoke twice, each time for a different purpose. The first is recorded in verse 43, "He cried with a loud voice, Lazarus, come forth."

How tense the atmosphere must have been, as every eye looked into the darkness of the open cave! What apprehension must have filled many hearts when they saw a figure wrapped around in long bandages struggling to walk to the mouth of the tomb.

Lazarus was alive, with all the potential of his renewed humanity, but he was powerless to move.

Then the Lord cried again, "Loose him, and let him go" (v. 44), and as the graveclothes were removed Lazarus was free to fulfill the new life he possessed.

This can be seen as an illustration of the three types of men in the world today. First, the many who are spiritually dead, locked in the tomb of sin, just as Lazarus was laid in the cave.

Then there are those who are born again. They have "come forth" from the tomb of sin, but, knowing nothing of the fullness of God's salvation, they stand with all the potential of their new life, still bound by the graveclothes of the old life. I meet many believers who go on through life clutching their graveclothes around them. They have never been set free from old habits, old sins, old life-styles, and these trip them up just as an old trailing garment could do.

What they need to hear is the second cry of the Lord, "Loose him, and let him go!" When they yield their lives to the risen Christ, turning from all their old behavior patterns, then he can move in, take over, and control, and his life is seen anew in their daily walk. "As ye have therefore received Christ Jesus the Lord, so walk ye in him." The same thought is seen in John 8:31-32, "Then said Jesus to those Jews which believed on him [notice that these words were addressed to believers], if ye continue in my word, then are ye my disciples indeed. And ye shall know the truth, and the truth shall make you free."

One further blessing is seen in relation to the other sister, Mary. Seemingly, Martha was always busy working. Lazarus was the one who was sick. But notice one lovely thought regarding Mary—she was always seen at the feet of Jesus.

"BELIEVEST THOU THIS?"

In Luke 10:38-42 we meet Martha "cumbered about much serving" (v. 40), but verse 39 says "she had a sister called Mary, which also sat at Jesus' feet, and heard his word." Because she sat, she heard.

In John 11:32 we read, "Then when Mary was come where Jesus was, and saw him, she fell down at his feet, saying unto him, Lord if thou hadst been here, my brother had not died."

John 12:1-3 records the supper that was made for the Lord after the raising of Lazarus. In verse 3 we find this lovely account, "Then took Mary a pound of ointment of spikenard, very costly, and anointed the feet of Jesus."

This supper presents the whole family involved with the Lord Jesus. We read, "Martha served" (v. 2)—that is stewardship; Lazarus . . . sat" (v. 4)—that is fellowship; "Mary . . . anointed" (v. 3)—that is worship.

Taken altogether, the three members of the lovely family present a composite picture of the life of a true, dedicated believer—stewardship, fellowship, and worship.

Now, as this chapter closes, do you have any answer to the question of the Lord, "Believest thou this?" Maybe something new has come to your mind, or some past experience has been reawakened, or some new door has opened, showing you a new life in Christ. If there is a response in your heart, why not follow through and first give joy to the Lord by your willing obedience? Then set yourself free in a new world as Christ becomes your life day by day—the hope of glory!

A Prayer for Meditation

My Blessed Lord, Thank you for the story of Lazarus and the graveclothes. I can see myself in this situation.

I have been born again by your wondrous death on the cross, and for this I thank and praise your holy name.

Now, Lord, I pray that you will call me forth and help me to be free from my old behavior pattern. Lord, loose me and let me go!

Help me to go on to receive all the blessings of your indwelling Spirit. May I learn to say in truth and reality, "For me to live is Christ." I ask this for your glory and through your precious name.

13.
"Why Do You Worry About The Rest?"

Surely this question from the Lord is one most needed in our world today. "Why do you worry?" We are learning one sad fact from today's pursuit of materialism: the more things you possess, the greater is your capacity for worry.

In Luke 12:15-31 the Lord was dealing with the whole question of materialism. He told the story of the rich man who planned to pull down his barns and build greater because of his success. He was planning for future security. "But God said unto him, Thou fool, this night thy soul shall be required of thee: then whose shall those things be, which thou has provided?" (v. 20).

He was successful by the world's standards, satisfied by his own standards, but sentenced by God's standards.

The repeated use of the word *things* in the following verses emphasizes the area of danger, "For all these things do the nations of the world seek after; and your Father knoweth that ye have need of these things. But rather seek ye the kingdom of God, and all these things shall be added unto you" (vv. 30-31).

Four times in this section in Luke's Gospel the Lord puts his finger on the problem and the danger. The *New International Version* says, "Do not worry about your life" (v. 22). "Who of you by worrying can add . . . ?" (v. 25). "Why do you worry about the rest?" (v. 26). "Do not worry about it" (v. 29).

Worry is first of all a spiritual problem. The tragedy is that it can develop into a mental problem which, in turn, can become a physical problem. Statistics in Britain show that 75 percent of the beds in hospitals are occupied by people who have put themselves there through worry.

By strange contrast, people in underdeveloped countries escape this modern illness. The scarcity of things removes the pressure to possess.

In this chapter I want to share with you God's plan for handling worry. If you follow, and "trust and obey," you could be opening new doors in your life which could lead into what Proverbs 3:17 says, "Her ways are ways of pleasantness, and all her paths are peace."

The Promise of Peace

Look with me then in Isaiah 26:3-4, and find one of the richest promises in God's Word, "Thou wilt keep him in perfect peace, whose mind is stayed on thee: because he trusteth in thee. Trust ye in the Lord for ever: for in the Lord Jehovah is everlasting strength."

Make sure you realize the certainty of this promise. Keeping you in perfect peace can only be on one condition, that your mind is stayed on the Lord.

One may be sceptical about claiming such a promise, seeing that it is written in the Old Testament. Let me give you a key which will open all the promise doors in the Bible. Look in 2 Corinthians 1:20 and read, "For all the promises of God in him are yea, and in him Amen, unto the glory of God by us." The *New International Version* says, "For no matter how many promises God has made, they are Yes in Christ."

In this remarkable verse the Holy Spirit tells an amazing truth— that every promise made by God can be realized in our lives through the person and work of the Lord Jesus Christ. And so the promise offered in Isaiah 26:3-4 can be yours, in Christ.

First, let us think again of that word *worry*, so common in many lives today, and its twin, *anxiety*. In one sense, worry is a sin. In Romans 14:23 we read this great definition, "For whatsoever is not of faith is sin." Worry is what develops when I tackle a situation on my own, in my own strength. When I choose to "go it alone," leaving God out of the situation, I am operating without faith, and thus worry and anxiety are sins.

Someone will say, "But if things go wrong, you have to feel something about the situation. If you must not worry, what is the alternative reaction?" This is a good question and opens up the subject in a fuller way.

In order to find the correct answer, we need to know one more thing. The Bible has much to say about the human heart; many verses refer to the "heart of a man." What does the Bible mean when it talks about the heart of a man? Certainly it is not referring to the physical organ which pumps the blood around the body. The obvious meaning is not physical but psychological.

The heart of a man is the man himself, his personality. I believe the Bible teaches that this is a trinity, composed of the emotions, the mind, and the will. Psychology teaches the same thing, using different words to name the three areas.

The Lord Jesus said, "Let not your heart be troubled" (John 14:1) and "Let not your heart be troubled, neither let it be afraid" (John 14:27). In Matthew 11:29 he said, "For I am meek and lowly of heart." These and similar verses tell us that the emotions are found within the heart.

Mark 2:6 says, "But there were certain of the scribes sitting there and reasoning in their hearts." In verse 8 the Lord asked them, "Why reason ye these things in your hearts?" In Luke 2:35 the old man Simeon speaking to Mary said, "That the thoughts of many hearts may be revealed." From these and other verses we understand that the mind is included in the term "the heart of man."

Now, using this information, that the heart includes both the emotions and the mind, let us look at the question we considered before. "If we must not worry, what is the alternative reaction?" The answer is that we should not worry, but we should be concerned.

Worry takes place in the mind. It is a confusion in the thinking process, resulting from failure to handle a situation.

On the other hand, concern is an emotional involvement resulting not from failure to handle a situation, but from a loving spirit wishing to help.

Isaiah 26:3 rules out worry entirely. It states, "Whose mind is stayed on thee." The mind in question is not seeking to handle the situation itself. It is committed to the Lord.

We can see a perfect illustration of the difference between worry and concern if we examine the behavior of the Lord in John 11:4, the story we considered in the previous chapter. Verses 33, 35, and 38 tell what happened when the Lord met Mary in all her brokenness, "When Jesus saw her weeping, and the Jews who had come along with her also weeping, he was deeply moved in spirit and troubled. "Jesus wept." "Jesus, once more deeply moved came to the tomb" (NIV).

Verse 35, the shortest verse in the Bible, simply states, "Jesus wept." It is interesting to find that the word used here for "wept" in the Greek is *dakruo*. It means to shed tears, and it is used only this once in the whole Bible.

We can understand immediately that the Lord was not worrying over the situation. He was concerned, very concerned, as shown by the tears he shed.

There was no need for worry. He knew that in the next few moments he was going to raise Lazarus from the dead. I find this concern of the Lord for these dear ones most moving, a lesson we need to learn. He had time to weep before he opened the floodgates of joy.

This brings us back to the question asked by the Lord, "Why do you worry?" We should be concerned about the problem but not worried!

Isaiah 26:3, "Thou wilt keep him in perfect peace, whose mind is stayed on thee." The only way in which my mind can cease from worrying is when it is stayed on the Lord. What does that mean? How can my mind be stayed upon the Lord?

The mind is that part of me which processes the thoughts that enter. Thoughts that are too many, too big, or too confused are more than the mind can handle. The answer is to find a way to control the thoughts that move in to cause that trouble.

The Bible gives us the answer if we look in 2 Corinthians 10:3-5. In this section Paul is telling of the problems and the battles he had to face, "For though we walk in the flesh, we do not war after the flesh. (For the weapons of our warfare are not carnal, but mighty through God to the pulling down of strong holds;) Casting down imaginations, and every high thing that exalteth itself against the knowledge of God, and bringing into captivity every thought to the obedience of Christ."

The secret of controlling thoughts that cause worry and anxiety is to bring these thoughts to Christ and let him permit or deny entrance to the mind. In this way the mind is stayed on Christ, trusting him to control what enters, trusting him to keep out all that could cause a buildup of worry or anxiety.

A similar process is illustrated for me each time I go to a foreign country. Having passed through immigration, I then must pass a customs officer who has every right to examine all my luggage. If he does, he is looking for items that are not allowed into that country. For example, when I fly from England to California, the customs officer asks whether I have any fruit. The reason is to prevent plant diseases from entering the country. In New Zealand the object is to keep out hoof and mouth disease in animals, and so the questions asked are whether I have been on a farm where cattle were. If I have been, then my footwear is taken and disinfected.

Thus, "Bringing into captivity every thought to . . . Christ" is to see him as the customs officer at the gateway of my mind. As the thoughts seek to enter the kingdom of my mind, he is in control, allowing or denying. My mind is now stayed on Christ, trusting him to handle the various situations as they arise.

Obviously, having the mind stayed on Christ is the task of a lifetime. There will be no sudden flash of victory, but a gradual sense of control will emerge as we take time to practice the presence of Christ.

In the previous chapters, we have discussed the technique for making Christ real in our lives. The problem is recognized, the difficulty is confessed, and the whole situation yielded to the Lord, as I openly admit, "Lord Jesus I can't handle this, but you can. Here and now, I want to yield the problem to you. I want to claim your promise that you will give me peace if I will keep my heart stayed on you."

The Power for Peace

In this chapter so far we have been considering the promise of peace. Now I want us to move on and think of the power for peace. The message continues right on from the previous paragraph.

We will find the power for peace in the same chapter, in Isaiah 26:12, "Lord, thou wilt ordain peace for us: for thou also hast wrought all our work in us." Again notice the confident assurance that God will ordain peace for us. Once I have sought to follow the instructions above, to differentiate between worry and concern, to allow the Lord to act as customs officer to the kingdom of my mind, then I am ready to discover the power by which this peace can flood my soul.

One important fact is to recognize the word *Lord*, to understand the meaning, and to respond to its claims. I have heard some people in prayer using the word only as a term of affection, "Dear Lord." The word denotes ownership. If he is my Lord, then I am his slave. It is his privilege to command; it is my duty to obey.

Once I understand this and stop making my own decisions, then the way is open for blessing. Notice the significance of the words in verse 12, "Thou wilt ordain peace for us: for thou hast wrought all our works in us." The power for peace comes from the One who works in us.

To the believer, this is speaking of the indwelling Christ. The same idea is found in Philippians 2:12-13. Notice again the sense of obedience and respect for authority, "Wherefore, my beloved, as ye have always obeyed, not as in my presence only, but now much more in my absence, work out your own salvation with fear and trembling. For it is God which worketh in you both to will and to do of his good pleasure."

These words in Philippians present the proper perspective about who does what in my life. Some would say that I should struggle on until I can do no more then hand it over to the Lord. The other extreme theory says I do absolutely nothing; I leave it all to the Lord to do everything.

The proper balance is achieved as I work out my own salvation; but all the time it is God who is working in me both to will and to do. It is his privilege to plan and also to perform. It is my duty to present my body a living sacrifice, as a tool in the hands of the One who is in control.

Paul puts it this way in Colossians 1:29, "To get this done I toil and struggle, using the mighty strength that Christ supplies, which is at work in me" (TEV). Paul was truly working it out unto weariness, but it was the Lord who was working in him.

This brings us once more to these two wondrous parts of the work of Christ in the salvation of the sinner. First there is his saving death, when he died for me, and by his precious shed blood he redeemed me. This is the finished work of Christ. Then there is his saving life, as he indwells me by his Holy Spirit. In his death it is Christ for me; in his saving life it is Christ in me.

It is this aspect of his work in me and through me which is emphasized in each of these three Scriptures: "Wrought all our works in us" (Isa. 26:12); "God which worketh in you" (Phil. 2:13); "He so mightily enkindles and works within me" (Col. 1:29).

Thus the power for peace is a reality, but I will experience it only in as much as I allow my Lord to work in me and through me.

The Program for Peace

So far we have discussed the promise and the actual possibility of peace in our daily lives. We have examined the power whereby that peace is produced. Now we need to see the program for peace, how it is to be worked out day by day.

We can see this by looking once more in Isaiah 26 but, this time, considering verses 13 and 14, "O Lord our God, other lords beside thee have had dominion over us; but by thee only will we make mention of thy name. They are dead, they shall not live; they are deceased, they shall not rise; therefore hast thou visited and destroyed them, and made all their memory to perish."

I find these two verses very remarkable in the depth and intensity of their teaching.

Notice how they begin, "O Lord our God." When we apply these words to the life of the believer, once again we are faced with the lordship of Christ. As we found before, this denotes the basis on which all these promises operate. It is his privilege to command in my life; it is my duty to obey. Immediately we come up against the most common reason for failure in our lives. We want to make our own decisions. Something in us resists the idea of being a slave. We believe in democracy, rule of the people. We fail to see that democracy is unscriptural. The correct form of government is theocracy, which means a direct government by God.

Those two verses are talking about the past in the life of the believer, using very vivid pictures. The verses speak of the other lords who controlled our lives, the habits, the sins, the waywardness, the selfishness, the lust. All these and many more were like masters in our lives, to whom we responded with slavish obedience.

Maybe we were not aware of our bondage. Maybe the chains were of silver or gold, but the fact remains that so many of us had lifestyles which were nothing more than bondage to the lusts of the flesh, however pretty or putrid they were.

But as these verses speak of the lords who ruled in the past, the whole emphasis is, "They are dead, they shall not live; they are deceased, they shall not rise; therefore hast thou visited and destroyed them, and made all their memory to perish." The language is emphatic. Not only are they dead, they are gone. Not only are they gone, but even their memory has perished. Here is a glorious sense of final freedom, as Charles Wesley wrote:

> Long my imprisoned spirit lay
> Fast bound in sin and nature's night;
> Thine eye diffused a quickening ray—
> I woke, the dungeon flamed with light;
> My chains fell off, my heart was free,
> I rose, went forth, and followed Thee.

This is the program for peace, or what I call the death of the past!

At this very point many believers have their biggest problem. They know their sins are forgiven; they know they have a home in heaven. But even so, they are haunted by the past, in thought, word, and deed.

If you are one of the many whose chains have not yet fallen off, let me show you truths to enable you to bury the past and go away and forget it.

Look with me at 1 John 1:9. This verse is, in a sense, the believer's declaration of independence from sin and self. "If we confess our sins, he is faithful and just to forgive us our sins, and to cleanse us from all unrighteousness."

This tells me that if I will do one thing, then God will do two things. The one thing I have to do is to confess my sins, not excuse them or rationalize them, not expiate them or condone them. My part is to own up and to acknowledge my sin, just as David did: "I acknowledge my transgressions: and my sin is ever before me. Against thee, thee only, have I sinned, and done this evil in thy sight" (Ps. 51:3-4).

If I do this one thing, God, in return, will do two things on my behalf. He will do these two things because he is both faithful and just.

Because he is faithful, he will forgive all my sins. The death of Christ has paid the price for that forgiveness. Now, here is the most important part for you who are still in our chains. When God forgives your sin, it is gone. There is no record left in heaven; when God forgives he forgets.

Not only is God faithful, he is just—because there is no record in heaven. He then goes on to cleanse you from all stain and guilt. Thus there is no divine record in heaven or on earth, as Isaiah 26:14 said, "They are dead, they shall not live; they are deceased, they shall not rise: therefore thou hast visited and destroyed them, and made all their memory to perish."

You may say, "Well, I am still troubled at times by what I have done. I still feel guilty." May I ask you, Who do you think is causing these feelings and thoughts to arise in your mind? Is it God, who has forgiven and forgotten? Is it Christ, who died to pay the price for your sin? Obviously the answer is No, in each case. Then, who is responsible?

Can you not see that it is the devil who is responsible for disturbing your peace? The last thing he wants is to see the believer at peace, resting in Christ. By stirring up the past he hopes to neutralize you so that you are no use to God in your disturbed state. What witness can you have when you are uncertain in your own soul?

These are some of the thoughts you bring to Christ as he sits at the customs post in your mind. Let him deal with them.

And so as your mind is stayed on Christ you appropriate the promise for peace. You gladly release the power for peace, and you daily follow the program for peace. This is the normal Christian life, as God planned it.

You must learn to say, "Thank you, Lord Jesus, because I have confessed these sins, they are gone. You have caused their memory to perish. May this be true in my own life. Help me always to refer these troublesome thoughts to you, and leave them there. Thank you for the peace of God which passes all understanding."

A Prayer for Meditation

Heavenly Father, Thank you for this promise of peace. Thank you, Lord Jesus, for your challenge concerning worry.

This has spoken to me directly. Help me to become involved in the way you teach. Help me to handle my worries. May I learn to turn worry into concern.

As I learn to rest in you, may my chains disappear and may I appreciate more and more the privilege of knowing you as my Lord.

14.
"Will You Also Go Away?"

It is a common practice now to use the rise and fall of a graph to indicate the measure of success in business sales and in popularity polls.

If such a graph were drawn showing the "success" in the life of the Lord, one of the high points would surely be the feeding of the five thousand. We read this account in John 6:1-15. The response of the multitude was unanimous. "Then these men, when they had seen the miracle that Jesus did, said, This is of a truth that prophet that should come in the world. When Jesus therefore perceived that they would come and take him by force, to make him a king, he departed again into a mountain himself alone" (vv. 14-15).

This was the kind of leader they wanted, someone who could bring instant healing to the sick and suffering, someone who could bring instant feeding to the crowds—the perfect welfare state. They were all eager to follow him and join his party.

But then, as our chapter unfolds, the Lord told them the price of following him and joining his group. It is this lesson which is so necessary today in many churches. It is human nature to want to jump on the band wagon, to join the winning party, to identify with success. Just as it is in business and politics, so often it is in religion.

This story in John 6 puts everything in its place. The Lord is still seeking people to follow him, still calling people to join his "party," but it is on his terms. We need to know what his terms are, so that we will be his followers not only in word, but in deed.

The enthusiasm of the crowds is seen in the way they searched for Jesus and followed him. Verses 24 tells how "They also took shipping, and came to Capernaum, seeking for Jesus." Just think of the activity on the lake of Galilee as crowds of people were ferried over to Capernaum. All business and private affairs were forgotten as these eager people actively pursued their "King."

In verses 26 and 27 the Lord began to put things in their proper perspective, "Ye seek me, not because ye saw the miracles, but because ye did eat of the loaves, and were filled. Labour not for the meat which perisheth, but for that meat that endureth unto everlasting life."

They were still willing to join his party, so they asked the leading question, "What shall we do, that we might work the works of God?" (v. 28). They were still interested, so they asked for a work schedule.

The Lord answered with words that had tremendous significance then and for all time, "This is the work of God, that ye believe on him whom he hath sent" (v. 29).

Make sure you notice that they wanted a list of works to do, but the Lord gave them just one thing to do, "Believe on him whom he hath sent."

This answer of the Lord immediately set the priorities in order. His list was so simple—just one thing to do, to believe on Jesus. It was so difficult—because all our other priorities then have to be reevaluated.

We have seen earlier in this book that to believe on Jesus is more than giving assent to certain historical facts. It is to receive him into our hearts and lives as our own personal Savior.

Thus, if the work of God is simply to believe on Jesus, to receive him, then this must be a daily activity, promoting a constant relationship. It is this very idea that the Lord developed as he continued in his teaching.

The crowd showed where their real interests lay by asking, "What sign shewest thou then, that we may see, and believe thee? what dost thou work?" (v. 30).

Verse 31 almost sounds as if they were asking for some more "bread from heaven to eat." It was feeding time once more!

The Lord then began his tremendous teaching concerning "the true bread from heaven." "For the bread of God is he which cometh down from heaven, and giveth life unto the world" (vv. 32-33). The crowds were still with him as they reached out, saying, "Lord, evermore give us this bread" (v. 34).

At this point the Lord began to press the challenge which eventually culminated in the collapse of their interest and their support. It is this challenge we need to face in our daily lives. "And Jesus said unto them, I am the bread of life: he that cometh to me shall never hunger; and he that believeth on me shall never thirst" (v. 35).

Suddenly the situation began to change. The Lord was not talking about baker's bread you could eat, but about himself as the Bread of life.

Notice now how the atmosphere began to change: "The Jews murmured at him, because he said, I am the bread which came down from heaven. And they said, Is not this Jesus, the son of Joseph, whose father and mother we know?" (vv. 41-42).

I find it very moving to read how the Lord gently, but deliberately, spelled out the cost of doing "the work of God." As we shall see, the crowd began to turn against him and, humanly speaking, he threw away all his chances of consolidating his successes as he presented the challenge of the truth.

In verse 43 the Jews murmured at him, but worse was to follow, as the Lord pressed home his great claim, "I am that bread of life. . . . I am the living bread which came down from heaven" (vv. 48,51a). Disregarding their reference to Joseph and Mary, he established his heavenly origin.

Then came the words which changed everything. "If any man eat of this bread, he shall live for ever: and the bread that I will give is my flesh, which I will give for the life of the world" (v. 51b).

By now they were completely out of their depth, and their murmuring changed to striving. "The Jews therefore strove among themselves saying, How can this man give us his flesh to eat?" (v. 52). Vine's Expository Dictionary says of the word *strove* that they began to fight, to quarrel, to dispute.

Relentlessly, the Lord continued as he placed the challenge before them, "Except ye eat the flesh of the Son of man, and drink his blood, ye have no life in you. For my flesh is meat indeed, and my blood is drink indeed. He that eateth my flesh, and drinketh my blood, dwelleth in me, and I in him. As the living Father hath sent me, and I live by the Father: so he that eateth me, even he shall live by me" (vv. 53,55-57).

Here then was the cost of joining his party, the price of becoming a true follower of Jesus. This is where the message speaks to us today.

The crowd was perfectly happy to be occupied with Jesus, to be where the action was, and live on the receiving end of the welfare relationship, but now the challenge had come. The Lord did not want them only to be occupied; he demanded identification with himself. The perfect illustration he used was the act of eating himself. We have personal relationship with the physical food we eat. We are completely identified with it. It becomes part of us and reaches into every area in our bodies.

I remember once seeing a Moody Science Film which showed dramatically this very fact. Dr. Moon was seen holding some food on a plate. This food was in some way impregnated with a harmless chemical which reacted to a microphone. We were shown that as the microphone was placed near the food a loud crackling was heard from speakers set up at the rear.

Dr. Moon told us he was going to eat this food, which would then go to his stomach and into the blood stream. The blood would then carry the chemical reactor to his heart. From there, it would be pumped to every part of his body.

He said he would hold the microphone in his hand so that when the chemical reactor came through his blood to his fingers the microphone would sense the arrival and the speakers would crackle, indicating that fact.

Behind him was a large clock with a second hand. We would see how long it actually took from eating to crackling. I must confess that when I heard Dr. Moon announce this experiment, I looked at my watch and wondered whether I had the time to wait!

As soon as he ate the food, the second hand began ticking away. The entire audience was silent. All we could hear was the click, click of each passing second.

To our utter and complete amazement, before the hand had reached twenty seconds we heard the crackle from the speakers. It was unbelievable to think that it took less than twenty seconds for the food to go from his mouth to every part of his body. We are indeed "fearfully and wonderfully made" (Ps. 139:14).

Not only does the food reach into these areas in a wonderful way, it becomes part of our body. We are literally what we eat, the various constituents doing their own special work in maintaining our health and strength.

If we eat poor food we will be undernourished. If our diet is unbalanced, we will show this in our physical appearance. If we eat poisonous food, we will be ill and may possibly die.

So the lesson taught by the Lord was perfect in every way. As I feed on him, allowing him to enter and influence every part of my life, then I will enjoy and reflect all the spiritual vitality of his risen life.

This is why in John 14:19 the Lord could say to his own, "Because I live, ye shall live also." He was not speaking only of life after death, but of life after life. That is the new life that is ours as believers here and now. As his life is allowed to bring nourishment, strength, and power to our lives, we have new resources for living day by day.

We have noted the reaction of the crowd to Christ's challenging teaching. First they murmured; then they strove among themselves. Their whole reaction was totally negative.

There were also many disciples gathered with the Lord at that time. These were not only the apostles, the chosen twelve, but others who had joined his party and had become recognized followers.

Verse 60 gives us the reaction of these disciples. "Many therefore of his disciples, when they heard this, said. This is a hard saying; who can hear it?" As we can see, they were repulsed by the message. All they could think of was the physical act of eating, and to apply that to a human body was utterly objectionable.

So the Lord spoke further, in verse 63, giving the obvious application of the truth, "It is the spirit that quickeneth, the flesh profiteth nothing: the words that I speak unto you, they are spirit, and they are life." Here he was underlining the spiritual nature of the eating, the feeding, and the drinking.

Verse 66 gives the subsequent action of their disciples, "From that time many of his disciples went back, and walked no more with him."

How quickly the graph has plummeted down. First the Jews have gone; now some of the disciples depart; and what was once a vast, enthusiastic crowd has given way to a small handful of waiting men.

Then it was that the question was asked which is the title of this chapter. Turning to the twelve the Lord asked, "Will ye also go away?" (v. 67).

Back came the tremendous answer of Peter, "Lord, to whom shall we go? thou hast the words of eternal life. And we believe and are sure that thou art that Christ, the Son of the living God" (vv. 68-69).

Notice that Peter did not ask, "To what shall we go?" but, "To whom shall we go?" He was affirming that the answer to life is not involvement with things, but a relationship with a person, the Son of the living God.

This is where we can pause and take stock of our own response to the offer of the risen Christ. "He that eateth my flesh, and drinketh my blood, dwelleth in me, and I in him" (v. 56). Realizing that this is a spiritual feeding on Christ, we can do one of three things. We can be like the enthusiastic crowd which, when the excitement stops just fades away. We can be disciples who really follow Christ, but when demands are made upon our faith we choose to rationalize and blame the Lord for making it so complicated. Third, we can be like the disciples who chose to stay with Christ and learn from him.

There will be some reading these words who genuinely want to "feed on Christ." Their question is very simple: "How do I feed on Christ?"

Let me take time now to be very practical and explain two essential things that must be in your life if you mean business. In John 8:31-32 we read these encouraging words, "Then said Jesus to those Jews which believed on him, If ye continue in my word, then are ye my disciples indeed. And ye shall know the truth, and the truth shall make you free." These words were spoken to believers who meant business. They form a kind of progression: continuing in "my word"; "disciples"; "know the truth"; freedom. Remember disciples are people who come under discipline, who accept discipline.

Christ here refers to continuing in his word. When we talk about the Word of God we are referring to two separate words. There is the written Word, the Bible. There is the living Word, the Lord Jesus himself, designated so in John 1:1: "In the beginning was the Word, and the Word was with God, and the Word was God."

Feeding on Christ is continuing in the Word.

First, let us consider the absolute essential of feeding on the written Word, the Bible. I find it a most remarkable thing that believers will read any number of books about the Bible. They will study the archaeology and geography of the Bible—especially if this includes a visit to the Holy Land itself. But getting down to the "word by word" study of the Book itself is a task often avoided.

I have listened, almost with amusement at times, to the reasons given for not studying the Bible. In the age of abounding leisure time, they have no time to study. In this age when a college education is a

"WILL YOU ALSO GO AWAY?"

benefit possessed by so many, they cannot understand it! The plain truth is "If we want to we will. If we don't want to we won't."

For years I have been encouraging people to discipline themselves to study. After all, a disciple is one who accepts discipline. If you want a method, here is the one I use. To do this you need a Bible, a notebook, and a writing implement. Each day you open your notebook and put the date on the next writing space. It is to be a daily study. I always begin with a psalm or part of a psalm. Write down the reference; then read your portion with an expectant heart. Ask the Lord to give you a thought, a phrase, a word, possibly tying your verse in with another verse elsewhere. You will find a concordance a great help in tracing the missing verses. The whole point of this exercise is to write down something under each reference. If the Lord sees you mean business, he will surely bless your study.

Having begun with a psalm, then go on to other sections in the Bible. I know no written rules for this, but for myself I read in two other Old Testament books and one New Testament book—four readings in all.

You read on day by day. When you encounter a section previously studied, start all over again. In this way, through the days, weeks, months, and years you will build up your own "Daily Devotions." As the years pass, you can look back and see how the Lord has spoken to you. The secret is to write something under each reference, if it is only copying out a phrase.

The time spent on "feeding on the Word" depends upon your own enthusiasm. Never say you do not have the time. Some real warriors have a motto, "No Bible—no breakfast."

As you read, let the Word speak to you personally. You are not building a library; you are feeding on the Word—so make it personal. If the Spirit challenges you through the Word to respond to his teaching, then, by his grace, let him work in your heart and life. You may not see many mighty changes in your life, but they will be there as you grow in grace.

You will find that feeding on the written Word is your job for life! Remember, if you lose your spiritual appetite and forget to feed on God's Word your life will show it. Remember, too, that the devil will do all he can to stop your devotions. "The Bible will keep you from the devil—or the devil will keep you from the Bible!"

I said before I wanted to be practical and to show you two ways in which you could "feed on Christ." We have just seen one very practical way—feeding on the written Word. Now let us consider the second way—feeding the living Word—Christ himself.

As we consider this most of all important area of our living, we go back to what has already been taught in previous chapters.

We have seen the twofold gift God offers to us in our salvation—the saving death of Christ and the saving life of Christ.

Salvation by his life is the continual present tense of our salvation, where he is allowed to finish in the crises what he began on the cross.

Feeding on the living Word, then, is maintaining a relationship with the risen Christ as he indwells me by his Holy Spirit. It is a relationship where he is Lord and I am his willing slave. He is King on the throne in my life. This is not just pious talk but a real and practical life-style, whereby each day I recognize his presence and yield my life to him for that day. If there are problems, temptations, fears, or any other situations where I am out of my depth, my immediate action is to yield it to him, telling him so, and thanking him for what he is going to do for me. Then I go on into the future, expecting nothing but blessings, even if I cannot see it, or understand it. I remember always that "God is able to make all grace abound toward you; that ye always having all sufficiency in all things, may abound to every good work" (2 Cor. 9:8). Always be thankful: "Thanks be unto God for his unspeakable gift" (2 Cor. 9:15).

So let us finish with the question asked by the Lord Jesus. When many had deserted him he said, "Will ye also go away?" What will your answer be?

Prayer for Meditation

Blessed Lord, I am really "on the spot"! I cannot turn my back on you and go away, and yet the challenge to "feed on you" is so demanding.

Help me, Lord, to see this not as a demand, but as a privilege—that I have the unspeakable honor and privilege of meeting you in your Holy Word day by day and the added honor of living with you hour by hour.

May these two opportunities become my rule for the rest of my life, not of blind duty, but of willing and glad surrender.

15.
"Why Weepest Thou?"

In this final chapter I want us to look at a woman of whom very little is said, or written, in our churches today. I feel I am almost writing in defense of her, because through the ages she has been maligned, misunderstood, misrepresented, and sometimes denigrated in a most unworthy, undeserved manner.

She is known as Mary Magdalene because she came from Magdala, which was a town in Galilee on the shores of the Sea of Galilee. Some tradition suggests she was a wicked woman with a sinful past, especially with regard to men. There is no justification for this, as we shall see. But somehow, if enough mud is thrown, some of it is bound to stick—and this is what has happened with Mary Magdalene.

The name Mary comes from the Hebrew word *Marah or Mara*, which means bitterness. In Ruth 1:20 Naomi cries out in her sorrow, "Call me not Naomi, call me Mara: for the Almighty hath dealt very bitterly with me." The name Naomi means pleasant.

There are six women in the New Testament called by the name Mary. Most important is, obviously, Mary the mother of the Lord. She was certainly a woman into whose life much bitterness came.

To begin with, she heard glorious words from the angel Gabriel telling about the future greatness of the Son she would bear: "He shall be great, and shall be called the Son of the Highest . . . he shall reign . . . and of his kingdom there shall be no end" (Luke 1:32-33).

She said, "My soul doth magnify the Lord, And my spirit hath rejoiced in God my Saviour . . . for behold, from henceforth all generations shall call me blessed. For he that is mighty hath done to me great things; and holy is his name (Luke 1:46-49).

But later on, in the Temple the old man Simeon would say to her,

"Behold, this child is set for the fall and rising again of many in Israel, and for a sign which shall be spoken against! (Yea, a sword shall pierce through thy own soul also)" (Luke 2:34-35).

How fearfully the sword pierced her soul! She heard all the promises of greatness and glory, but she saw very few of them come true. There came a day when she stood by the cross and saw her own precious, beloved Son die in agony. She well deserved the name of Mary.

Her name appears nineteen times in the New Testament. Mary Magdalene is mentioned fourteen times. By contrast the other Marys are just incidental. We can see right away that Mary from Magdala stands out as being an important character, if only on the basis of being mentioned so often.

I want us to consider her life in four separate time frames before she knew the Lord; in his life; at his death; in his resurrection. From these we can learn great lessons which could help us in our daily lives, especially in times of bitterness.

Before She Knew the Lord

No details are given of Mary's life before she knew Christ, but we can discover certain facts. There is no mention of a husband or children. This is most unusual, because marriage was the normal way of life and children were considered a blessing from the Lord. A single woman was in a precarious position in the Jewish society of those days, especially if she had no father; and there is no indication given of any relative in her life.

In His Life

In two passages we learn a very important fact about Mary in connection with the Lord. Luke 8:2 and Mark 16:9 both tell us that the Lord had cast seven devils out of her.

This is a terrifying story! For a person to be possessed and inhabited by one demon was bad enough. Realize the implications of this situation. It means that another personality lives in the same body. This experience is increasing in our society today as people choose to open up their lives to Satan and his diabolical influence.

Having another personality sharing the same body means that all the faculties of mind, emotion, and will, all the areas of spirit, soul,

"WHY WEEPEST THOU?"

and body are available to both persons. The demon can use the voice with which to speak, use, or abuse the body. He can take over the body and the mind and express his own evil personality—facially, physically, and emotionally.

All this happens today in America, in our modern society. No wonder such evil is experienced in the country.

It must be an agonizing position to be possessed by one demon, but imagine the ghastly situation where seven separate demons shared the one body with Mary. This actually meant that there were eight persons in that one body, each seeking to express themselves in every way possible. Of course, we shall see that when Jesus enters a life, the devils can no longer possess it. The best exorcism is the reception of Jesus into one's being. Satanic influences will oppose the Christian, but they cannot have dominion over or possession of the believer.

Mary Magdalene, before she met the Lord, may have been lonely, friendless—a creature of evil ways and uncertain habits, all of which had no relation to her own personality. She was locked in prison with seven demons.

This is why the day she met the Lord and he cast out those demons was for her the greatest, most wonderful day there ever was. One moment her body was a place dominated by wickedness. Then Jesus commanded, and the demons vanished, leaving Mary alone. There she was in possession of her own body, to do with as she chose for the first time.

Immediately she made her choice; her life from then on was dedicated to the service of the One who had set her free. We will find, as we go on, that she moved into a position vitally important to the ministry of the Lord.

The second thing we learn about Mary is the work she did. Luke 8:1-13 tells us how the Lord "went throughout every city and village, preaching and shewing the glad tidings of the kingdom of God: and the twelve were with him, And certain women, which had been healed of evil spirits and infirmities. Mary called Magdalene, out of whom went seven devils, And Joanna the wife of Chuza Herod's steward, and Susanna, and many others, which ministered unto him out of their substance" (vv. 1-3).

The same special information is given in Mark 15:40-41. This sometimes comes as a surprise to many people when they realize the important part played by this band of devoted women. We are told that wherever the Lord and his twelve disciples went, those women went with them. Their job was to help the disciples, cooking, washing, cleaning, mending, and whatever else might be necessary. Not only did they work, they also helped pay the bills!

The Lord and his band had no income. None of them were men of private means. Thus they were dependent on these few women for everything.

The leader of this support group was Mary Magdalene with all the rich devotion filling her newly released body. The first person she ever met in her new life was Jesus, and he became the only one in her life. It needs no imagination to think how she would lead the workers in their loving tasks—all for Jesus!

In His Death

If we stop and think how much the Lord meant to Mary Magdalene in her life day by day, we can imagine the horror and the shock that must have overwhelmed her when he died. Her whole world must have fallen to pieces. She might have thought she had nothing left to live for. She knew no real life apart from being with him in his ministry.

So we read in Matthew 27:55-56, "And many women were there beholding afar off, which followed Jesus from Galilee, ministering unto him: Among which was Mary Magdalene."

There she was, with the rest of her workers, just beholding afar off. She was powerless to help now, even though she wanted to. This was the end.

John the apostle was there when it happened, and this is what he wrote, "Now there stood by the cross of Jesus his mother, and his mother's sister, Mary the wife of Cleophas, and Mary Magdalene" (John 19:25). This is a most revealing passage. There were four women there with John, and three of them were called Mary—"Bitterness." We read in Matthew 27 that Mary Magdalene was standing afar off with her group. Now John tells us that as the end drew near Mary came and joined those intimate personal friends who were standing around the cross.

Here was her Lord and Master, the one she had loved and served so devotedly. Now he was dying, and Mary's life was fading before her eyes.

When Mary Magdalene was listed with her band of workers, her name was always first. Now John has a different order, and she is last.

There was a sacred relationship between Mary the mother of Jesus and the apostle John. He never mentions her by her name; he usually calls her "the mother of Jesus." This is seen in John 2:1,3,5,12; 19:25-26. Likewise he never names himself. He usually calls himself "the disciple whom Jesus loved" (see John 19:26; 21:7; 20,24). This special relationship was sealed at the cross. John 19:26-27 says, "When Jesus therefore saw his mother, and the disciple standing by, whom he loved, he saith unto his mother, Woman, behold thy son! Then saith he to the disciple, Behold thy mother! And from that hour that disciple took her unto his own home."

The word translated here "Woman" is a term of affection. A more meaningful translation is "Dear Lady."

I wonder why the Lord committed his mother to John when she already had other sons and daughters? Two of the sons wrote books in the Bible—James and Jude.

In Matthew 27:57-61 and Mark 15:43-47, we are told how Joseph of Arimathaea came and took the body of Jesus and laid it in his own new tomb. Matthew's account ends with the pathetic picture of "Mary Magdalene and the other Mary, sitting over against the sepulchre" (v. 61).

Life for Mary was where Jesus was and even in his death she was near him—a most moving scene.

In His Resurrection

Mary saw where the body was laid, and then she departed, because the sabbath began at sunset on Friday. I wonder what she did the next day, her first day of separation from the Lord she loved? Each Gospel tells us that very early on the Sunday morning she went back to the tomb, with a friend.

Her desire was to care for his body in death. She was carrying spices which they had prepared. With these she would have anointed his body and given it a sweet fragrance to dispel the odor of death.

Even as she was on her way, "There was a great earthquake: for the angel of the Lord descended from heaven, and came and rolled back the stone from the door" (Matt. 28:2).

And so dawned the day of resurrection, the day of the risen, victorious Christ, the day of the empty tomb.

But Mary knew nothing of this. Her heart was broken, and her hands were full of spices as she continued on her way to show her love to her Lord.

John 20:1-18 is a section full of rich and glorious truth. We read in verse 1 how Mary came and saw the stone taken away. Verse 2 tells how she ran to tell Peter and John. This, incidentally, is the only place in the Bible where a woman is depicted as running.

Verse 4 continues with Peter and John running to the tomb. Notice the running and the physical activity on this Easter morning.

Verse 5 tells how John looked into the empty tomb. Verse 6 tells of Peter going into the tomb and seeing the linen clothes lying. In verse 8 we read how John went in, "and he saw, and believed."

In the King James Version the word "see" is used in each case to describe the visual act of Mary and Peter and John. But in the original, three different words are used. When we understand the meaning of each word the whole section becomes richer in significance.

When Mary "saw," the word is *blepo*. This is the ordinary act of seeing. Verse 5 tells how John "saw" from outside the tomb. This also is the word *blepo*.

Peter went in and "seeth the linen clothes lie, And the napkin, that was about his head, not lying with the linen clothes, but wrapped together in a place by itself" (vv. 6-7). The word "see" there is *theoro*. This implies he looked at the sight critically and carefully.

John saw the same sight and "he saw, and believed." The word used for "saw" is *eido*, which means he understood. We sometimes use the same idea; we say, "I see what you mean; I understand what you mean."

What was it they saw in the tomb that made Peter stop and think, but led John to believe that Jesus was actually risen from the dead?

The information is in the description of the position of the clothing in the tomb. In those days the body was wrapped round and round, using long, wide bandages, with spices in between to counteract the smell of corruption. The head was wrapped around in a towel. This

"WHY WEEPEST THOU?"

was how the body of Jesus had been treated by Joseph and Nicodemus (John 19:39-40).

But at the moment of resurrection his body became a new body, a resurrection body, capable, as we know, of entering a room even when the doors were locked.

This resurrection body passed through all the folds of the bandages, through the towel "wrapped together in a place by itself," leaving them still folded but empty. This is what John saw, and in a flash, he realized what had happened.

This incident is one of the glorious proofs of the actual physical resurrection, written by an eyewitness who told it as he saw it. There was no other way in which the bandages and towel could be left still rolled and all in place.

Each Gospel tells the story of the resurrection with its own special emphasis. There is a lovely thought in Mark 16:9 concerning Mary Magdalene, "Now when Jesus was risen early the first day of the week, he appeared first to Mary Magdalene, out of whom he had cast seven devils."

The Lord Jesus chose to appear first to Mary—not to his important disciples who would one day be the heroes of the early church, but to this lonely, forsaken woman. I find this most comforting, so like the Lord. His priorities are so different from those of the world. The broken heart of a lonely woman was the most important need at that time.

We saw above, in John's Gospel, how John and Peter had run to the empty tomb at the instigation of Mary. After the incident of John's seeing and believing we read in verse 10, "Then the disciples went away again unto their own home."

The following verse is deeply moving, "But Mary stood without at the sepulchre weeping" (v. 11). The two men returned, as it said, to their own home, but Mary had no home to which she could go. Her home, since her deliverance, had always been where Jesus was, but now he was dead. All she could do was to stay where she last saw his body and wait, and weep, and wonder.

The story continues, telling us how she stooped and looked into the tomb once more, hurting herself again as she saw just the empty graveclothes. Even the sight of the two angels was no shock to her. Nothing was greater than the tragedy she was then experiencing.

They asked her why she was weeping. She said, "Because they have taken away my Lord, and I know not where they have laid him." She had a new question. Who were "they" who had taken away her Lord? She had accepted the fact of his death. All she wanted to find now was his dead body.

Then came a moment which must have thrilled the angels in heaven. Suddenly she turned and saw someone standing in front of her. It was the risen Christ, but her head was bowed in grief. Her eyes were swollen with weeping, and she failed to recognize him.

He asked her those memorable words, "Women, why weepest thou? whom seekest thou?" (v. 15).

She, poor, lonely soul, thought he was the gardener: "Sir, if thou have borne him hence, tell me where thou hast laid him, and I will take him away" (v. 16). She would take him away. How lovely, how impossible, how sincere, but, oh how unnecessary!

The risen Christ said one word, "Mary," and the floodgates of joy burst open wide as she cried out in glad and glorious surprise, "Master" (v. 16).

Then the Lord said some words to her which should have great significance for us today. The King James' Version says, "Touch me not" (v. 17). A better translation is, "Don't cling to me."

As we have seen throughout her story, her one aim in life had been to care for the Lord, to serve him. This was not only true in his life, but especially so in his death. She had been quite prepared to spend the rest of her life keeping alive the memory of a wonderful Savior who died on the cross.

"But," says the Lord, in effect, "Not so. Don't cling to me. From now on you will need a new relationship with me" (AT).

The new relationship was to be with the risen, victorious Christ, who, after Pentecost, would come and indwell her through his Holy Spirit. From then on, she could be a new kind of servant.

The question heading this chapter is, "Why weepest thou?" Perhaps you are reading these words and you, too, feel lonely, downcast, as if you had no future. Do you know the risen Christ? Or are you clinging to a Savior who died on the cross, with nothing more to come, except a far-off hope of heaven?

The answer to every need in every heart, whether broken or unbroken, lonely or wandering, is to get your eyes on the risen, victorious Christ. Call him "Master," as Mary did, and then move off into a new and living relationship which will never end. Discover all the riches in the saving life of Christ, and your tears will turn from sorrow to joy.

Prayer for Meditation

Thank you, my Master, for this story of Mary Magdalene. May I see you, with the eyes of faith, in all your risen power, and so may my life never be the same again.